CW00346152

Rely on Thomas Cook as your travelling companion on your next trip and benefit from our unique heritage.

Thomas Cook **pocket** guides

MARRAKECH

Written and photographed by Ethel Davies
Updated by Maryam Montague & Chris Redecke

Published by Thomas Cook Publishing
A division of Thomas Cook Tour Operations Limited
Company registration No: 3772199 England
The Thomas Cook Business Park, 9 Coningsby Road
Peterborough PE3 8SB, United Kingdom
Email: books@thomascook.com, Tel: +44 (0)1733 416477
www.thomascookpublishing.com

Produced by The Content Works Ltd
Aston Court, Kingsmead Business Park, Frederick Place
High Wycombe, Bucks HP11 1LA
www.thecontentworks.com

Series design based on an original concept by Studio 183 Limited

ISBN: 978-1-84848-280-7

First edition © 2006 Thomas Cook Publishing
This third edition © 2009 Thomas Cook Publishing
Text © Thomas Cook Publishing
Maps © Thomas Cook Publishing/PCGraphics (UK) Limited

Series Editor: Lucy Armstrong
Production/DTP: Steven Collins

Printed and bound in Spain by GraphyCems

Cover photography (Mint tea) © SIME/Moscheni Francesca/4Corners Images

CONTENTS

SYMBOLS KEY

The following symbols are used throughout this book:

🄰 address 🄣 telephone 🅦 website address 🄲 opening times
🅝 public transport connections 🄘 important

The following symbols are used on the maps:

𝒊	information office	▦	points of interest
✈	airport	◯	city
✚	hospital	◯	large town
🛡	police station	○	small town
🚍	bus station	=	motorway
🚆	railway station	—	main road
❶	numbers denote featured	—	minor road
	cafés & restaurants	—	railway

Hotels and restaurants are graded by approximate price as follows:
£ budget price ££ mid-range price £££ expensive

Abbreviations used in addresses:
av.   avenue
blvd   boulevard
pl.   place

▶ *Gate in traditional oriental style near the Royal Palace*

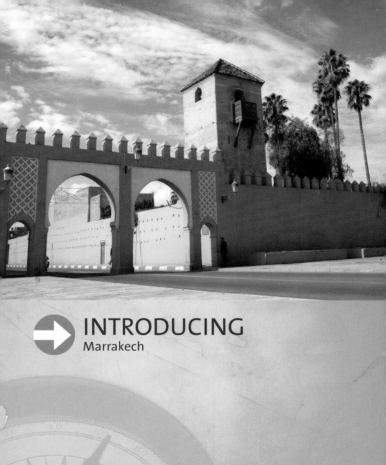

INTRODUCING
Marrakech

Introduction

The first thing that a visitor to Marrakech notices is the colour of the city. Everywhere seems to be a salmon-shade of dark pink, whether on the houses of the recent developments near the airport, 21st-century office blocks or the buildings of the old city. Marrakech, the capital of south Morocco in spirit, if no longer in name, is painted the colours of the sub-Saharan desert sands. It is said that each new construction is allowed a choice of only two colours: the pinker hue of the city's historical hotel, the Mamounia, or the slightly more ochre version of the Koutobuia, the tall, graceful minaret that is Marrakech's landmark.

The next thing that becomes apparent to visitors is the wall surrounding the old city, or Medina. High and still intact, with massive gates placed at intervals along it, this impressive edifice separates the modern European metropolis from the ancient Arab one. UNESCO declared this ancient enclave a World Heritage Site in 1985, in order to guarantee its preservation.

The new city, with more modern areas such as Guéliz and Hivernage, has broad tree-lined boulevards, a legacy left by the French, who occupied Morocco for 44 years. Meanwhile the old city is surrounded, seemingly keeping its secrets inside. It's the sense of these mysteries that makes Marrakech so appealing and, inside the Medina, the labyrinth of streets and passageways adds further confusion. There is a logic to the ancient Medina, however, and the locals are friendly, so it doesn't matter if you get lost – sooner or later you'll find your way.

Just inside the walls is the Jemaa el Fna. A UNESCO 'Heritage of Humanity' site, this huge square is filled with Moroccan characters, selling their wares or demonstrating their skills. At night, the place is packed with locals, clamouring to hear tales from the storytellers as well as watch the various ethnic performers. Dozens of food stalls with benches for diners are packed in against one another, each with its hawkers soliciting passers-by for customers. Further in, it's impossible not to get caught up in the various markets, or souks. Shopping is an experience that's dazzling to the eye, as well as to the pocket.

Not all of the city's population lives inside the densely packed old centre. The new city is growing almost daily, with suburbs springing up in surrounding areas and plans to increase the urban development further.

Beyond the official city limits is the Palmeraie, once a palm grove and now the most fashionable resort area (see page 111). With exclusive hotels, luxury houses, a golf course and horse riding, this suburb is where both the domestic and foreign wealthy are choosing to build their second homes.

On clear days, especially during the winter, the natural barrier against which the entire region nestles becomes visible. The High Atlas, North Africa's highest mountains, lie just to the south of Marrakech. Mount Toubkal, at 4,165 m (13,665 ft), is the tallest peak in the north of the continent and it's possible to ascend to the summit in a mere couple of days. There are also other destinations in the area that make this region an easy single- or multi-day excursion away from the city.

If being inland in a country with such a long ocean coast is a problem, the seaside resort of Essaouira makes a welcome change from the dry sands of Marrakech. 170 km (105 miles) from Marrakech (two hours by bus or taxi), this easygoing blue-and-white city is known for its battlements, fresh fish and artistic atmosphere.

When to go

Spring and autumn are the most pleasant seasons to visit Marrakech, as the weather is at its gentlest during these times of year. The summer months of July and August are very hot. To attend the city's most important folk event, the Festival of Popular Arts (see page 12), however, you have to brave the heat of July. Even the relative coolness of winter is pleasant compared to Northern Europe, although it can rain quite a bit. In the colder months the air is clear, and snow on the Atlas presents a spectacular backdrop to the city, which can be skied upon at the mountain resort of Oukaïmeden. It is best to avoid travelling during the holy month of Ramadan (see page 12), as many restaurants are closed by day (except for those in some hotels) and stores have erratic hours.

SEASONS & CLIMATE

Located in the plains below North Africa's highest range, springtime is pleasant, with temperatures on average in the mid-20s °C (70s °F). There can be some precipitation during the earlier part of the season, although plants and flowers flourish in the rain. Summers are hot and dry, with the thermometer reaching about 38°C (100°F) during the day, and rarely going below 20°C (68°F) at night. Rising haze obscures visibility and can last into the autumn, although the temperature drops back down into the 20s °C (70s °F) as the year progresses.

In the winter, clear days offer spectacular glimpses of the snow-covered Atlas Mountains. Although not warm by Moroccan standards, at an average of 17°C (62°F), and with darker and wetter days than the rest of the year, winter in Marrakech can still be a pleasant break for Northern European or American visitors.

ANNUAL EVENTS

Morocco has many celebrations and festivals throughout the year, some intended only for Muslim worshippers and some with more international appeal. Most events taking place in Marrakech and the surrounding area are fun to join in with and offer visitors a unique insight into Moroccan culture. However, do check the dates of Muslim festivals carefully as they generally follow a lunar calendar and can be unpredictable. Ramadam, for instance, begins when the first sliver of a new moon can be seen by the local Imam – it is not actually calculated scientifically and the date varies from year to year (see page 12). During Ramadam Muslims adhere to very strict regulations regarding eating, drinking and

● *A taste of Fantasia festivities at Chez Ali (see page 112)*

entertainment. As a holidaymaker this might be a good month to avoid.

A good source of information on events taking place in Marrakech is Ⓦ www.marrakechpocket.com

January

Marrakech Marathon With Morocco producing champion long-distance runners, the Marrakech marathon attracts thousands of participants. Ⓦ www.marathon-marrakech.com

February

Dakka Marrakchia Festival This festival takes its name from a genre of music that is typified by multiple percussive rhythms and chanting. Local artisans come to participate, to honour the Sabaatou Rijal, the city's spiritual guardians.

May

Friendship Festival This biennial festival takes place in even-numbered years, usually over three days, and gathers together musicians of all types and nationalities to celebrate the benefits of living harmoniously.

June

Gnaoua Festival A four-day music festival held annually in Essaouira (170 km/105 miles west of Marrakech, see page 135). It is dedicated to the traditional *Gnaoua* style of music and dance and is attended by both music lovers and internationally known performers. Ⓦ www.festival-gnaoua.co.ma

---

▶ *Activities at the Festival of Popular Arts are held in El Badi Palace*

July

Marrakech Festival of Popular Arts The city's most important folklore event celebrates traditional Moroccan cultural forms and includes singing and dancing. Events take place across the Medina, but are centred on El Badi Palace, which is packed with performers, dancers and those being entertained for the duration of the folk festival. Most spectacular of all is the display of horsemanship at the Fantasia (see page 38), held every night of the festival just outside the city walls near Bab Jdid.

Montreux Jazz Festival Morocco The world's most prestigious jazz fest is now being marketed across the globe, and the Marrakech version is a great showpiece for local artists, who get to play alongside established greats. Ⓦ www.montreuxjazz.com

August

Festival les Calèches Each year the French bring a wide range of performers to Marrakech to show the locals what they think *le vrai rock'n'roll* is all about.

Imilchil Marriage Festival This event, which sees as many as 50 couples get married at the same time, is more than just a big Berber knees-up: it allows eligible singles to check out the talent and in time, perhaps, keep the tribal traditions alive.

Setti Fatma Moussem Although this *moussem*, or pilgrimage to a holy shrine, is dedicated to the saint Setti Fatma, this event in the High Atlas villages (see page 120) is more of a fair than a religious event.

August–October

Ramadan For a period of one month, Muslims adhere to the restrictions of Ramadan – no eating, smoking, drinking or sexual activity from dawn till dusk. Most restaurants outside of hotels are closed by day. The last day is known as Eid El Fitr.

November & December
The Marrakech International Film Festival (see page 14).
Eid al-Adha Festival This Muslim celebration of piety is marked by colourful ceremonies in mosques all over the city, and by the ritual slaughter of farm animals.

PUBLIC HOLIDAYS
Muslim holidays (*) can vary by as much as a month, as they are based on the lunar calendar.
New Year's Day 1 Jan
Fatih Mouharram (Islamic New Year) Around 10 Jan*
Aïd al-Mawlid (The Prophet's Birthday) Around 20 Mar*
Labour Day 1 May
Throne Day 30 July
Oued Eddahab Allegiance Day 14 Aug
Revolution Day 20 Aug
The King's Birthday 21 Aug
Ramadan For 30 days from around 11 Aug 2010, 1 Aug 2011, 20 July 2012*
Eid El Fitr Last day of Ramadam
Green March Day 6 Nov
Independence Day 18 Nov

Marrakech International Film Festival

The Marrakech International Film Festival may still be relatively young, but it's made it on to cinema's 'A' list. Attracting famous actors from all over the world, the event claims it is a meeting point of East and West. In practice, it is more of a North African Cannes, with glamour, parties and even royal patronage, as shown by King Mohamed VI's sponsorship and keen interest.

Since its opening in the autumn of 2001, the festival has gone from strength to strength. Juries have been presided over by well-known Western personalities such as American directors Roman Polanski and Martin Scorsese and the English director Alan Parker. Additionally, honours have been given to the Scottish actor Sean Connery and German director Dominik Graf. African filmmakers are also represented, both by their presence and their work, and the cinema of the Far East is also shown. These days, more and more mainstream cinema interests are becoming involved. The festival is now held in November, spilling over into December.

Marrakech itself is the venue. When audiences are too large for the Colisée Cinema or the Palais du Congres, outdoor screens are set up in the grounds of the enormous ruins of El Badi Palace, as well as the huge square of the Jemaa el Fna. All films are presented in their original versions with French, Arabic and English subtitles. As the festival gains in popularity, and its audience continues to increase beyond the 100,000 who already attend, more of the city will be used as impromptu exhibition areas.

Movie-going is a popular form of entertainment not just during the festival but throughout the year. Comfortable, modern cinemas abound in the city, including Cinéma Rif, La Colisée and Mégarama Theatre (see page 110). For something a little less mainstream, check out the French Cultural Institute (see page 101).

Cinema has long been important to Morocco. Hollywood discovered that the scenery of the country could double for other, less accessible, locations, and began to come in order to start making movies. In 1952 Orson Welles arrived in Marrakech's seaside neighbour of Essaouira, where he made his film *Othello*. This event, and the director himself, were commemorated in the naming of one of the city's squares as place Orson Welles. A few years later, Alfred Hitchcock decided to use the Hotel Mamounia in his movie *The Man Who Knew Too Much*. The turning point in Morocco's career as a film set really came in 1962, when David Lean chose its desert as the location for *Lawrence of Arabia*.

Since then, movies have been made here on a regular basis. Morocco stands in for any number of places, such as Israel in *Jesus of Nazareth*, an unnamed Middle Eastern country in *Jewel of the Nile*, somewhere in Asia Minor in *Alexander* and even Tibet, in Martin Scorsese's film of the life of the Dalai Lama, *Kundun*. Further south and closer to the real desert is the town of Ouarzazate. Here, a film studio grows ever larger, hosting bigger and bigger productions. The latest movie to be shot in Marrakech and Ouarzazate is *Prince of Persia: The Sands of Time*, based on Ubisoft's action-adventure computer game of the same name. Between the cheap labour available from both technicians and extras, the political stability and the government's (and the aforementioned King's) sympathy towards the industry, making movies here is a real alternative to production in more expensive places. It's not surprising that more and more of the films shown in the Marrakech International Film Festival, whether of African origin or not, were actually filmed in Morocco.

For more information on the festival, see Ⓦ www.festival-marrakech.com.

History

Marrakech has always been a city of Berbers, an ancient assembly of members of unknown Euro-Asiatic origin, residing primarily in the Atlas Mountains. The history of the area comprises a continual wave of invasions from both internal and external powers. Yet the heritage remains to this day, with about 75 per cent of the population descended from Berber tribes.

When the seagoing Phoenicians first arrived on the Atlantic coast in the 12th century BC, the Berbers were already well established,

and they remained the main racial group throughout subsequent foreign incursions. By this point, the region had become a spot of rich pickings, as it held an important position on the trade routes between central Africa and the sea coast. The early history of Morocco can seem like a series of raids by visiting conquerors such as the Romans, Byzantines and Arabs.

In the 11th century, a group of Berber tribes banded together to form the Almoravids. Strong, resilient and used to the harsh

The magnificence of the Saadian rule is apparent in the tombs of their princes

conditions of mountain life, the group set up camp at the base of one of the major crossroads of the Atlas Mountains. This settlement became a fixed point on the trade route, and became known as 'Marra Kouch'. Historians do not agree on the meaning, but one possible explanation is 'the Land of the Kouchmen' (a tribe of black warriors from Mauretania, the country that once included Morocco as one of its territories). Adhering to the Muslim faith that most Berbers had adopted during the Arab conquests, the Almoravids began to expand into adjoining lands and soon had an Islamic empire that reached as far as Lisbon to the north, West Africa to the west, Algeria to the east, and all of Morocco to the south. The capital Marrakech flourished and became a magnificent city, although all that remains of this glory today is the Qoubba ablutions pool (see page 68).

The city's history began to follow a pattern, with one tribe conquering, flourishing, developing the city, going into decline and then falling to the next invaders. The Almohads in the mid-12th century were next, first defeating the Almoravids, then destroying the old Marrakech but rebuilding a beautiful one in its place. Many of the city's current structures, including its icon, the graceful minaret of the Koutoubia (see page 75), were built at this time. By 1276, however, the last of the Almohads were overcome by the next ruling tribe, the Merenids.

Marrakech was out of favour with the Merenids, however, and the new imperial cities of the north, including Fez, took precedence. This decline continued until the Merenids, weakened by internal issues and continual Christian attacks from the Iberian Peninsula, were overwhelmed by the next tribe, the Saadians, in the mid-16th century.

The ruling sultans returned to Marrakech, moving the court and reinvesting in the city, and it began to blossom once more. Arts and architecture flourished, and many details still visible today sprang from this era. However, after the death of the Saadian sultan in 1607, chaos returned. For more than 60 years civil war raged, until an Arab prince arrived to settle the conflict. Though his reign was not marked by anything particularly notable, he created a bloodline that remains, indeed his descendants rule Morocco today.

Marrakech remained virtually medieval until 1856, when the sultan Abdel Rahman, anxious to modernise his nation and afraid of France's intentions, signed a free-trade agreement with Britain. His signature effectively opened up Morocco to Europe, bringing it into the 19th century, but also priming it once again for conquest. For the next 60 years, France continued to encroach upon the country till finally, in the Treaty of Fez in 1912, the sultan bowed to pressure and allowed Morocco to become a colony of the French.

Subjugation was always going to be tricky, and despite seemingly enlightened policies such as choosing representatives from local people, and significantly modernising the Marrakech landscape, being under foreign rule was hard for the Moroccans. When the numbers of resident Europeans became enormous, and the gap between lifestyles too much to take, the seeds of an independence movement were sown. In 1953, the anxious French sent Mohammed V into exile, an event that further riled the nation. A period of violence ensued and the King was allowed to return in 1955. By then, however, governing the colony was just too difficult, and France granted Morocco independence in March 1956.

As a constitutional monarchy, with Mohammed V's son, King Hassan II, the first modern ruler of the independent country of Morocco, the country began to stabilise. Today, Hassan II's son, King Mohammed VI, is on the throne. Mohammed is seen as a moderniser, and his priority is to continue the country's development up to 21st-century standards while alleviating its serious poverty issues.

Lifestyle

Marrakech is exotic, and the mystery and secrecy of life behind its walls applies to its culture as well as to its buildings. Women walk in the streets in all variations of garb, whether in a Muslim head scarf or wearing low-slung jeans. Or both. Morocco is a Muslim country, effectively and legally. With the exception of a small number of Jews, everyone born here is Muslim and must adhere to Islam's tenets. In theory, for example, flaunting of the restrictions of Ramadan (see page 12) can mean imprisonment, though this rarely actually happens. Islam is avidly followed, but not generally in a fundamentalist way. The call to prayer is broadcast from various minarets throughout the city five times

● *Traditional Arabian carpets line the streets as they dry after being washed*

a day, the first between 04.15 and 05.00. Often the slightly different timings create a strange, not quite echoing, song, with the varying pitches and voices overlapping. Nondescript doors that are closed most of the time are opened during prayer times, and, for non-believers, it's possible to catch a glimpse of reverent men bowing on their prayer mats just beyond. Mosques, it should be noted, are not open to non-Muslims.

For all this reverence for traditional ways, foreigners are accepted and welcomed, indeed allowances are made for tourists where they might not be for locals. For example, the wearing of long shorts and going around with bare shoulders is just about tolerated for visitors, but rarely seen among Marrakchis. However, do use discretion when dressing: respect is certainly something that the Moroccans appreciate.

For all its aspirations and plans, Morocco is still pretty much a developing country. Be sure to only drink bottled water and remain cautious when eating street food (the stalls at the Jemaa el Fna are an exception, as they are generally licensed). Almost all streets in the Medina have now been paved, but you should still take care not to trip. Many people are poor, especially in the countryside, and illiteracy is still a serious issue. Even those children lucky enough to go to school – and the number is up to almost 50 per cent for girls – usually finish their education by the age of 13.

What seems expensive to a local appears cheap to Western tourists. Prices are low here and goods and services cost relatively little. Many visitors come for extended periods, finding their money lasting longer than they expected. Alternatively, it's also possible to buy a lot more in the souks. Eventually, though, the weight or bulk restrictions of carrying all one's purchases might limit buying power more than the price!

Culture

From the mass of people gathering to watch performances in the old city's main square to the exquisite artistic detailing suddenly appearing out of nowhere on the walls, Marrakech is a city of the arts. The Medina's huge open area, the Jemaa El Fna (see page 73), is the location of daily expressions of Morocco's living culture. Here is where you'll find people engaging in lively street performances and dances, day and night.

Upholding old traditions while continuing to enthral each new generation is one of Marrakech's most important cultural legacies. The fundamentalist Islamic belief that art should be representational rather than realistic has led to a plethora of beautiful abstract creations, and these can be found in many locations throughout the city. Old royal residences like the Bahia Palace (see page 68) are covered with such forms and have now been turned into museums. The Saadian Tombs (see page 80) are surprisingly cheerful, with magnificent mosaics and superb wood carvings surrounding the outdoor graveyard.

Some private buildings have been converted to areas open to the public, such as Bert Flint's home, now the Tiskiwin Museum (see page 82), and the Ben Youssef Medersa (see page 70). Other exhibitions worth a visit include the Dar Si Said Museum (see page 81), the Marrakech Museum (see page 83) and the Museum of Islamic Arts (see page 102) hiding within the exquisite Le Jardin Majorelle (Majorelle Gardens, see page 98).

The Théâtre Royal (see page 101) in Guéliz in the new city is a beautiful home for much of Marrakech's performing arts, and the

---

● *The Bahia Palace is filled with typical representational designs*

Philharmonic Orchestra of Morocco uses the hall as its Marrakech venue. Cinema is very popular, with several good movie theatres in the new city (see page 110) catering to the populace's wish to see films from both Hollywood and the rest of the world. The Marrakech International Film Festival (see page 14) acknowledges the country's adoration of the medium. Other celebrations occur regularly, including the Festival of Popular Arts in July.

Art can be found in several areas of the souks (markets), with many craftsmen producing work that rises above the general tourist kitsch. More formally, however, some Moroccan artists are represented in art galleries across the city. Places such as La Qoubba Galerie d'Art (see page 87) in the Medina and the Matisse Art Gallery (see page 101) in Guéliz present contemporary works in appropriate surroundings. More casual and less pretentious is the Ensemble Artisanal (see page 83), not far from the town hall, a series of workshops used by traditional craftsmen.

Although Moroccan music is internationally acknowledged, much of it in association with Western rock (Jimmy Page and Robert Plant have recorded with Gnaoua musicians), there are almost no regular venues in Marrakech to hear it performed. The Jemaa has its share of musicians, although many of them stop and start according to the number of coins thrown at them.

Although you must pay to visit Marrakech's galleries, museums and palaces, you'll be pleasantly surprised to find that admission fees are very low.

● *Marrakech's icon is the minaret of the Koutoubia mosque*

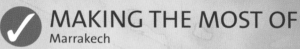

MAKING THE MOST OF
Marrakech

Shopping

One of the very best things to do in Marrakech is to go shopping. Whether you're simply having a browse or are harbouring serious purchasing intentions, shopping here is fun; in fact it's possible to visit the city and do nothing else.

Souks are defined as 'marketplaces in northern Africa or the Middle East', and the ones in this city are some of the best in the Arab world. In the centre of the Medina are tiny maze-like streets made even narrower by the masses of goods on display. Seemingly chaotic, the different souks are divided and classified, more or less,

BARGAINING

Bargaining over the price of items is necessary in virtually all of the souk shops in the Medina. Prices are not marked and vendors will almost never give the best asking price of goods when first asked. A good rule of thumb is to offer an amount that is between one-third and one-half of the first asking price and then to negotiate upwards. In the case of carpets, fiercer haggling is expected and buyers should begin negotiations with an amount that is one-tenth to one-quarter of that price. When the seller refuses to lower the amount any further, the buyer may decide if the price is acceptable or, if still too high, walk away. If the seller does not follow the ex-buyer to negotiate further, then it's clear the final figure has been put on the table. So *caveat, emptor*, but enjoy the game while it lasts.

▶ *The sellers themselves bring character to the myriad city stalls*

by the goods they sell. The main marketplace is just north of the Jemaa el Fna, and some of the specialities include dried fruit and nuts (Souk Kchacha), carpets (Souk Joutia Zrabi), leather goods (Souk Cherratine) and dyed yarns (Souk Sebbaghine). Venturing further into the labyrinth, past the stalls, it's possible to wander into the areas where the craftsmen are working, producing the goods seen on display. Most of the markets are not fixed-price and bargaining is an essential part of the purchasing process. As a guideline, it's worth visiting some of the fixed-price crafts shops, such as the Ensemble Artisanal in the Medina, to find out

◆ With stalls specialising in one item, you are always spoilt for choice

USEFUL SHOPPING PHRASES

What time do the shops open/close?
A quelle heure ouvrent/ferment les magasins?
Ah kehlur oovr/fehrm leh mahgazhang?

How much is this?
C'est combien?
Cey combyahng?

Can I try this on?
Puis-je essayer ceci?
Pweezh ehssayeh cerssee?

My size is ...
Ma taille (clothes)/
ma pointure (shoes) est ...
Mah tie/mah pooahngtewr ay ...

I'll take this one, thank you
Je prends celui-ci/celle-ci, merci
*Zher prahng serlweesi/
sehlsee, mehrsee*

how much they charge for similar goods. Alternatively, if bargaining is not an option, it might be better to visit some of the more conventional, if ultimately more expensive, stores. Hidden within the souks are shops that offer finer and more exclusive goods than are seen on the outside stalls.

Guéliz in the new city also has its share of elegant shopping, where price tags are immovable and usually higher than in the markets. In Gueliz you will find shops offering high-quality handbags and other accessories, shoes, designer clothes, antiques and linens. Serious shoppers will head to the area of Sidi Ghanem, or the industrial zone, about a 20-minute drive from the city centre off the boulevard de Safi. There you will find large stores that furnish and decorate many of the city's luxury guesthouses.

Eating & drinking

Although Marrakech has a large number of restaurants – and even more cafés – there is not much variety in gastronomic styles. Food tends to consist of Moroccan specialities, with Italian dishes as an alternative (a few of the more exclusive restaurants offer fine French cuisine, and there are also Thai and Japanese eateries). As for vegetarian fare, it's possible to order dishes modified to be meatless, though it must be said that specifically vegetarian dishes are rare. Salads are a regular item on the lunch menu, though, as is the Moroccan vegetarian soup, *harira*.

If you fancy a truly authentic experience, eating at the stalls on the Jemaa el Fna Square is certainly worth doing at least once. All the food is cooked to order, based on whatever is on display, and some of these impromptu eateries have impressively wide-ranging menus.

There are no dress codes at any of the casual restaurants, and seating arrangements are pretty much do-it-yourself, too. At the evening Jemaa eating spots, for example, you simply sit down wherever there is space. The more elegant places will require more formal

PRICE CATEGORIES

The restaurant price guides used in the book indicate the approximate cost of a three-course meal for one person, excluding drinks, at the time of writing.

£ up to D180   ££ D180–500   £££ over D500

● *Kebabs may be had at a wide variety of eateries*

LOCAL SPECIALITIES

Moroccan cuisine is distinctive and delicious, if not terribly varied. Tagines, the best-known dishes, are stews of meat or chicken slow cooked and dressed up with apricots, prunes, raisins, citrus fruit, onions, olives or almonds (depending on the type), then served up with bread. The platter with a cone-shaped lid bears the same name. It's possible to see rows of these earthenware pots cooking away in many of the restaurants and stalls throughout Marrakech. Couscous, a kind of semolina ground into small kernels, is also on offer, especially on Fridays. The Moroccan soup, *harira*, made with tomatoes and chickpeas, is a delicious vegetarian alternative. *Harissa*, a spicy red tomato-and-varying-degrees-of-chilli sauce, is sometimes offered alongside Moroccan dishes to liven up the mix.

attire, although a suit and tie for men is never mandatory. At these places, the maitre d' will seat customers. Tipping is common at the more relaxed restaurants, the amount ranging from rounding up the bill to five per cent. At the posher venues, gratuities will usually be included in the total.

Many of the classier restaurants are open evenings only from around 19.00, although some open for lunch then close again until dinner; a number of these restaurants are closed on Mondays or Tuesdays, so reservations are advisable.

Morocco is a Muslim country and alcohol consumption is still largely frowned upon, but the number of places where drinks are served is growing. There are several places in the Medina where it's possible to get a drink at a bar, but it's easier to get hold of wine in connection with a meal at some of the more expensive restaurants. In general, liquor is more readily available in the French-influenced Guéliz and Hivernage, or the westernised Palmeraie, than in the Medina. But who needs booze when Marrakech has some of the

⬤ Tagine is both the name of the conical cooking vessel and of the dish itself

USEFUL DINING PHRASES

I would like a table for ... people
Je voudrais une table pour ... personnes
Zher voodray ewn tabl poor ... pehrson

Waiter/waitress!
Monsieur/Mademoiselle, s'il vous plaît!
M'sewr/madmwahzel, sylvooplay!

May I have the bill, please?
L'addition, s'il vous plaît!
Laddyssyawng, sylvooplay!

Could I have it well-cooked/medium/rare please?
Je le voudrais bien cuit/à point/saignant
Zher ler voodray beeang kwee/ah pwang/saynyang

I am a vegetarian. Does this contain meat?
Je suis végétarien (végétarienne). Est-ce que ce plat
contient de la viande?
*Zher swee vehzhehtarianhg (vehzhehtarien). Essker ser plah
kontyang der lah veeahngd?*

Where is the toilet, please?
Où sont les toilettes, s'il vous plaît?
Oo sawng leh twahlaitt, sylvooplay?

best orange juice in the world? The Jemaa el Fna is full of vendors selling freshly pressed juice, each one shouting for customers. The local drink of choice is mint tea. Brewed from daily deliveries of bunches of fresh mint and laden with almost more sugar than water, the beverage is a Moroccan institution. It is served at most hours, refreshing energy levels at midday and finishing a meal off nicely. It also serves as an aid to commerce, being brought out in the middle of a bargaining situation, or offered at its successful conclusion.

Coffee is an everyday drink, too, and is in plentiful supply. People-watching goes hand in hand with coffee consumption and the pavement cafés are always full of pleasantly caffeinated spectators. Locals come here to read the newspapers and chat with friends.

When the weather is fine, you may feel tempted to buy supplies at a souk or supermarket and eat outdoors. Marrakech is not an ideal place for picnicking, as food stores are not plentiful. The city is a bit dusty and the midday heat can get fierce, especially in summer. However, if eating on the green is a necessity, there are parks and gardens just beyond the city walls that have pleasant places to sit.

The stalls at the souks are excellent for dried fruit, nuts, olives and pastries, although more basic foodstuffs are available at the small local mini-marts situated throughout the city. Larger supermarkets are located in the new city, with **Acima** (🕻 05 24 43 04 53) in Guéliz and **Aswakasalaam** (🕻 05 24 43 10 04) near Bab Doukkala. On the city's outskirts, **Marjane** (🕻 05 24 24 31 37 86) can be found on the route de Casablanca and may be reached by taxi or car.

Entertainment & nightlife

The nightlife of the city is pretty divided, with the Medina providing more traditional, and for the most part more sober, forms of entertainment, while Guéliz, Hivernage and the Palmeraie supply the majority of bars, clubs and discos. The Islamic rules of no alcohol are not enforced for foreigners, but it's still easier to find drinks in the modern part of the city. The Jemaa el Fna is the centre of traditional night entertainment, but there are more formal and touristy versions at the dinner shows just outside of town. The national symphony orchestra comes to town periodically and it's possible to hear them

● *The Jemaa offers a magical setting for night-time crowds*

perform at the Théâtre Royal. Cinema is very popular and it can be a real experience to join locals in their deck chairs in the open-air, watching the latest blockbusters.

The best form of free entertainment is arguably the street life around Jemaa el Fna square. During the day this is a tranquil place, but crowds start to rush in from nowhere at around 18.00 and the atmosphere becomes suddenly charged with life. Stroll through the crowds listening to the cries of the merchants and the faux-plaintive bargaining, and watching the storytellers, dancers and musicians. If the noise and crowds get too intense, the cafés and restaurants around the square provide places to relax while looking on.

Relatively few places within the Medina offer alcohol. Outside

of the restaurants that serve wine with a meal, it's possible to get a drink at the (apparently ironically named) Grand Hotel Tazi (see page 45), a backpackers' hotel that has a cheap bar. On a more upmarket scale, the Café Arabe (see page 91) has a large terrace with a bar that is particularly lovely.

Guéliz in the new city is much better stocked with bars. Many are located along the main avenue, Mohammed V, and it's possible to get a drink here without any problem. In the nearby streets are other places as well, with both locals and visitors attending (and in many cases, accompanying trade). Discos are popular, most of them attached to hotels with predominantly foreign tourists. There are also

FANTASIA – CHARGE OF THE FIGHT BRIGADE

If you like your entertainment pitched at wow-factor ten, take a look at Fantasia. Despite the name, this is no Mickey Mouse affair, but a full-blooded display of machismo demonstrated through astonishing horsemanship. The spectacle, which is thought to have originated as a show-of-strength ritual among the Berbers in the harsh Rif Mountains to the north of Morocco, is a pageant of martial prowess that culminates in horsemen in traditional garb charging their steeds while firing rifles into the air and shouting. Subtle it is not; impressive it is. The safest and most reliable way to view Fantasia is at the annual Marrakech Festival of Popular Arts (see page 12), though somewhat sanitised versions are staged at **Borj Bladi** (ⓐ 57 rue Mauritania ⓣ 05 24 43 08 90 ⓦ www.borjbladi.ma) and Chez Ali (see page 112) in the Palmeraie.

some bars and clubs in the area of Hivernage. The Palmeraie, the trendiest location and a taxi-drive away from the centre, has developed a reputation as a party place. Some of the more fashionable clubs are here (see page 109).

Surprisingly, Marrakech also has a couple of casinos. In Hotel La Mamounia you'll find the **Grand Casino** (❶ 05 24 44 45 70), offering various games including blackjack, craps and roulette. The one at the **Es Saadi Hotel** in Hivernage (❶ 05 24 44 88 11) is not quite as fancy, but will take your money just the same. Although neither charges an entry fee, minimum stakes are pretty high. Casual attire is not permitted, and you might even lose your shirt.

While Marrakech is a wonderful place for ad-hoc street music, if you're looking for some sounds in a more formal context, you should hope that the Moroccan Symphony Orchestra will be in town when you visit. A good bet for music is the Jemaa el Fna. During the Festival of Popular Arts (see page 12) in the city or the Gnaoua Festival (see page 11) in Essaouira, it's possible to hear traditional musicians on a more organised basis than usual.

There are several cinemas in Marrakech. For the most comfortable film viewing, head to the new, nine-screen Mégarama. Two cinemas in Guéliz, La Colisée and Cinéma Rif, also play the latest films from Hollywood and the rest of the world (see page 110). Note that the versions are often dubbed into French and sometimes in Arabic. The French Cultural Institute (see page 101) on the route de Targa offers the opportunity to view Moroccan cinema, as well as arty films. Films are often subtitled in French.

To find out what's on, check out the free French-language publications *Marrakech Pocket* and *Tout Le Monde En Parle*, available in hotels and restaurants throughout the city. Another good resource is the website ⓦ www.marrakechpocket.com.

Sport & relaxation

The city and its environs have their fair share of sporting and leisure activities, mostly due to the amenable climate that allows opportunities all year round. Hammams, or public baths, are a Moroccan institution and appear in many different guises.

SPECTATOR SPORTS
Football
The resident soccer clubs, Kawkab and Najim, are based at the **El Harti Stadium** (ⓐ Jnane el Harti) in Guéliz. When there's a game on, it's usually possible to buy tickets on the day.

PARTICIPATION SPORTS
Golf
There are three courses in Marrakech, with three more opening in late 2010. Golf d'Amelkis has 27 holes. All golf courses charge around 500 dirhams for 18 holes.
Golf d'Amelkis ⓐ route de Ouarzazate ⓣ 05 24 40 44 14
ⓛ 08.00–16.00 summer; 08.00–14.00 winter
Palmeraie Golf Palace ⓐ Circuit de la Palmeraie ⓣ 05 24 30 10 10
ⓦ www.pgp.co.ma ⓛ 07.00–19.00
Royal Golf Club ⓐ Ancienne route de Ouarzazate ⓣ 05 24 40 98 28
ⓛ Sunrise–sunset summer; 09.00–14.30 winter

Hiking
Although this takes place in the High Atlas, the city is a good place to arrange excursions, if you haven't already done so. **High Country** (ⓦ www.highcountry.co.uk) and the Kasbah du Toubkal (see page 118) can help plan hiking trips.

HAMMAMS

Steeped in Moroccan tradition, hammams are public steam baths where the sexes are separated, and people come to get clean and relax. Their style and the quality vary, but they usually include two or three rooms, each progressively hotter than the last. Hot and cold water come from taps and visitors use buckets to pour water over themselves. Variations include body scrubs (known as *gommages*) administered by a professional scrubber, as well as massages.

Although there are hammams all over the city, three of the nicer ones are listed here:

Les Bains de Marrakech Stylish setting for major pampering.
ⓐ 2 Derb Sedra, Bab Agnaou Kasbah ⓣ 05 24 38 14 28
ⓦ www.lesbainsdemarrakech.com ⓛ By appointment

Hammam Ziani Simple but good value. ⓐ 14 rue Riad Zitoun el Jdid ⓣ 06 62 71 55 71 ⓦ www.hammamziani.ma ⓛ 07.00–21.00

Le Palais Rhoul Spa Splurge on an unforgettable experience.
ⓐ Dar Tounsi km 5, routes de Fès ⓣ 05 24 32 94 94
ⓦ www.palaisrhoul.com ⓛ By appointment

Karting & quad-biking

This sport has been soaring in popularity, with the semi-arid areas around the city proving to be excellent grounds for roaring around. **Atlas Karting** (ⓣ 05 24 33 20 33) and **Locaquad** (ⓣ 05 24 31 44 44 ⓦ www.locaquad.com) are two of the most reliable companies.

Horse riding

For a great day or half-day ride, including a picnic, try **Ben Sassi**

Ranch ( route de Fez, km 19 ☎ 06 15 28 57 28). Another good option is **Marrakech Cheval** (⊚ route de Casablanca, near Hotel Sangho ☎ 06 61 17 36 04).

Essaouira, two-and-a-half hours away from Marrakech, on the coast, offers horse and camel riding on the beach (see page 130).

Skiing

Seventy kilometres (43 miles) up the mountain in the High Atlas, when there's snow at the winter resort of Oukaïmeden, locals and tourists alike put on skis to use the chairlifts and downhill runs (see page 117). Serious skiers may find the trails inadequately challenging.

Swimming

The best options for taking a dip are at the few hotels that have pools and allow visitors to use the facilities for a fee:

Le Nikki Beach (in the Palmeraie Golf Palace) Offers swimming and club facilities for day use. Cocktails are also served. ⓐ Circuit de la Palmeraie ⓣ 05 24 30 10 10 ⓛ 11.30–18.30

La Plage Rouge Marrakech's biggest pool in a stylish setting, with a bar and restaurant. ⓐ route de l'Ourika, km 10 ⓣ 05 24 37 80 86 ⓦ www.ilove-marrakesh.com

● *Some of the best places for a little recreation are away from the city*

Accommodation

There are a phenomenal number of places to stay in the city, ranging from a campsite and youth hostel to some of the finest hotels in the world. In between are *riads*, a sort of boutique bed and breakfast-cum-guesthouse-cum-hotel virtually unique to Morocco. Mostly found in the Medina, these places are often unmarked and hidden, frequently requiring a walk through labyrinthine streets too narrow for cars. Originally private houses with courtyards, the residences were bought up, decorated and furnished to the purchasers' tastes. Quite a few have been acquired by Europeans, some who intended to move in and live full time, others who were looking for holiday or investment opportunities. As Marrakech began to become a fashionable tourist destination, these owners realised that they could rent out rooms. There are now over 600 *riads*, all with a relatively small number of rooms, and each a unique assembly of personal taste. Some of them are absolutely exquisite – with prices to match – and others are remarkably good value. There are even a few with swimming pools, although the restrictions of space within the cramped Medina make this a rarity. They all include breakfast, many offering beverages or afternoon snacks. Most can also arrange lunch or an evening meal,

PRICE CATEGORIES

The bigger hotels conform to a star, and the smaller hotels to a lantern, rating system, but as so many places to stay are individually owned, the designations have little comparative value. Prices for one night in a double room for two people are:

£ up to D800   **££** D800–2,000   **£££** over D2,000

either cooked on site or brought in from a local restaurant, effectively acting as room service. European-owned residences often provide alcohol. What proves to be a problem with *riads* is the same thing that makes them so desirable – their small size. The more popular ones soon fill up, so booking ahead is often essential.

Decent alternatives do exist, and there are some excellent hotels in Marrakech. Within the new city, the hotel chains, such as Ibis and Sofitel, are well represented. In the Hivernage area, there are numerous 4- and 5-star hotels. Medium-level hotels are also in Guéliz, for those visitors looking for something halfway between small *riads* and enormous hotels. Beyond, in the Palmeraie, are huge hotel resorts or luxurious palace hotels that are quite a distance away from the Medina, but offer full sport and leisure facilities as recompense.

If travelling independently, deciding where to stay can be difficult. The choices listed on the following pages are by necessity subjective and only a tiny selection. For more information check out the following websites: ⓦ www.riadsmorocco.com ⓦ www.ilove-marrakech.com ⓦ www.morocco-travel.com

HOTELS & RIADS

Dar Fakir £ This converted *riad* is beautifully furnished with large full-facility rooms. ⓐ 16 Derb Abou el Fadall, Medina (The Old City) ⓘ 05 24 44 11 00

Grand Hotel Tazi £ Hardly grand, this is one of the cheaper places to stay in the Medina. It's popular with backpackers, not just because of the price of the rooms, but also because of the cheap beer. ⓐ Corner av. el Mouahidine & rue de Bab Agnaou (The Old City) ⓘ 05 24 44 27 87

Hotel Ali £ Popular with backpackers again, this cheap and cheerful hotel is centrally situated and has a bureau de change and internet café. ⓐ rue Moulay Ismail, Medina (The Old City) ⓣ 05 24 44 49 79

Hotel Ibis £ Part of the economy branch of the Accor chain, this hotel is surprisingly nice, with a large pool, situated right next to the railway station. A new Ibis (ⓣ 05 24 33 40 20) has opened on the route to Casablanca in the Palmeraie. ⓐ av. Hassan II, pl. de la Gare, Guéliz (The New City) ⓣ 05 24 43 59 29 33 ⓦ www.accorhotels.com)

Hotel Islane £ An inexpensive hotel located directly across from the Koutoubia minaret; a good restaurant and excellent ice cream stand are on the premises. ⓐ 279 av. Med. V, Medina (The Old City) ⓣ 05 24 44 00 81

Hotel Sherazade £ One of the best-value small hotels in the Medina, the décor is simple but friendly. ⓐ 3 Derb Djama, Riad Zitoun el Kdim, Medina (The Old City) ⓣ 05 24 42 93 05 ⓦ www.hotelsherazade.com

Hotel du Trésor £ A haven for artists and design lovers, this beautifully converted small hotel, offers fantastic value for money. With Wi-Fi and a small heated pool, this place is ideally located near the Jemaa el Fna. ⓐ 77 Sidi Boulokat, Riad Zitoun el Kdim, Medina (The Old City) ⓣ 05 24 37 51 13

Morocco House Hotel £–££ Located in the middle of the new city, this friendly, comfortable hotel gives its guests a choice of 3-, 4- or 5- star accommodation. ⓐ 3 rue Loubnane, Guéliz (The New City) ⓣ 05 24 42 03 06 ⓦ www.moroccanhousehotels.com

Each riad – *Moroccan boutique hotel – has its own character*

La Maison Arabe ££ One of Marrakech's finest, and best-known small hotels, the restaurant – and cookery school – are also famous. ⓐ 1 Derb Assehbe, Bab Doukkala, Medina (The Old City) ⓣ 05 24 38 70 10 ⓦ www.lamaisonarabe.com

Maison Mnabha ££ This lovely *riad* in the Kasbah area of the Medina is English owned and run. ⓐ 32–33 Derb Mnabha, Kasbah, Medina (The Old City) ⓣ 05 24 38 13 25 ⓦ www.maisonmnabha.com

Riad 72 ££ The unique appeal of this *riad* is its lovely Italian-Moroccan design mix. It's located in the Medina, north of the Jemaa. ⓐ 72 Arset

Awsel, Bab Doukkala, Medina (The Old City) ☎ 05 24 38 76 29
🌐 www.riad72.com

Riad Saba ££ Centred around a delightful central courtyard, this *riad* is charming. The English-speaking Swedish and Moroccan owners are wonderfully friendly and helpful, and also run a travel agency, **Marrakech Travel Company** (🌐 www.mtravel.se) and may assist in planning your trip. ➌ 2 Derb Cherkaoui, Douar Graoua, Medina (The Old City) ☎ 06 62 83 98 29 🌐 www.riad-saba.com

Riyad el Cadi ££ Looking more like a gallery than a residence, this was once the home of the German ambassador to Morocco, an avid art collector. ➌ 87 Derb Moulay Abdul Kader, Derb Dabachi, Medina (The Old City) ☎ 05 24 37 86 55 🌐 www.riyadelcadi.com

Sofitel ££ Up to its usual luxury hotel standard, the top link of the Accor chain has a large presence just outside the Medina. ➌ rue Harroun Errachid, Hivernage (The New City) ☎ 05 24 42 56 00 🌐 www.accorhotels.com

Amanjena Hotel £££ Part of the luxury Aman resort chain, this is one of Marrakech's most beautiful hotels, often hosting movie stars and footballers. Located west of the Medina, the Amanjena is near two golf courses. ➌ route de Ouarzazate, km 12 ☎ 05 24 40 33 53 🌐 www.amanresorts.com

Jardins de la Koutoubia £££ Despite being right off the main square, this large modern deluxe hotel with huge pool is surprisingly quiet. ➌ 26 rue de la Koutoubia, Medina (The Old City) ☎ 05 24 38 88 00 🌐 www.lesjardinsdelakoutoubia.com

Le Palais Rhoul £££ Situated west of the Medina, this first-class accommodation offers sumptuous personalised care. Stay in one of the famed luxury tents for an unforgettable experience. ❸ Dar tounsi, route de Fez, km 5 ❶ 05 24 32 94 94 Ⓦ www.palaisrhoul.com

Palmeraie Golf Palace £££ An enormous complex north of the Medina, boasting a 27-hole golf course, horse riding, swimming pools (see page 43) and a luxury hotel. ❸ Circuit de la Palmeraie (The New City) ❶ 05 24 30 10 10 Ⓦ www.pgp.co.ma

Riad Lotus Privilege £££ Part of the group of Lotus hotels, this exquisite *riad* features stunning design and incredible décor. With a magnificent courtyard and small pool, this place is honeymoon worthy. ❸ 9 Derb Sidi Ali Ben Hamdouch, Medina (The Old City) ❶ 05 24 43 15 37 Ⓦ www.riadslotus.com

La Villa des Orangers £££ Another wonderful, luxurious secret hiding right behind the main square, the only Relais & Chateaux-rated hotel in Morocco also has a pool. ❸ rue Sidi Mimoun, Medina (The Old City) ❶ 05 24 38 46 38 Ⓦ www.villadesorangers.com

HOSTELS & CAMPSITES
Auberge de jeunesse £ The Marrakech youth hostel is located outside the Medina, in the Hivernage area of town. ❸ rue el Jahed, Hivernage (The New City) ❶ 05 24 44 77 13

Camping Ferdaous £ Marrakech's campsite is situated north of the city, close to the Marjane Hypermarket. ❸ route de Casablanca, km 13 ❶ 05 24 30 40 90

THE BEST OF MARRAKECH

Whether you are on a flying visit to Marrakech or have a little more time to explore the city and its surroundings, there are some sights, places and experiences that you should not miss. For the best attractions for children, see page 147.

TOP 10 ATTRACTIONS

- **El Badi** The ruins of an enormous royal residence dating from the late 16th century, this massive space has an awesome ambience and spectacular views of the High Atlas Mountains (see page 73)

- **La Bahia Palace** Ba Ahmed Ben Moussa's beautiful 19th-century palace filled with courtyards, gardens and exquisite detailing (see page 68)

- **Ben Youssef Medersa** Formerly a Koranic school, the courtyards flanked by what were once students' cells are full of magnificent examples of Hispano-Moorish decoration (see page 70)

- **City gates** The ancient entry points into the Medina through the city walls still have the power to impress (see page 70)

🔻 *Moroccan tagine pots come in a wonderful array of colours*

- **Hammams** The Moroccan version of a steam bath is often accompanied by a scrub with a special glove and a massage (see page 41)

- **Jemaa el Fna** This huge square has Moroccan street entertainment during the day and – even better – at night (see pages 36 & 73)

- **La Koutoubia** Marrakech's landmark is a graceful 12th-century minaret towering 77 m (252 ft) above the city with beautiful adjoining rose gardens (see page 75)

- **Le Jardin Majorelle (Majorelle Gardens)** Literally an oasis in the new town, the eponymous artist's lush exotic gardens were restored by the fashion designer, Yves Saint-Laurent (see page 98)

- **Souks** The inner city's markets are fabulous to look at as well as excellent places to buy a remarkable array of goods (see page 76)

- **Saadian Tombs** Graves of the dynasty's princes are situated in lovely gardens, enhanced by beautiful Moroccan representational art (see page 80)

Suggested itineraries

HALF-DAY: MARRAKECH IN A HURRY

Start at the Koutoubia (see page 75), then wander a bit further to explore the gardens that are close to the base of the tower. Turn back towards the Jemaa el Fna (see page 73) and spend some time watching the street performances and busy goings-on, before buying a glass of refreshing orange juice from one of the many vendors. Head north into the maze of souks and just wander, letting whim take hold. If the opportunity allows, drop in and visit the Bahia Palace (see page 68). Save a little time for a stop at a café in order to try a mint tea.

1 DAY: TIME TO SEE A LITTLE MORE

With a few more hours available, spend more time in the souks, perhaps ambling towards the smaller alleyways and backstreets to watch the craftsmen working. Continue north to visit the Ben Youssef Medersa (see page 70), buying the combined ticket that allows entry to the nearby Almoravid Qoubba and Marrakech Museum. While at the Medersa, make sure you go upstairs to see a few of the cells. Continue across the way to the impressive remains of the Qoubba, the washing pool of the Almoravid (see page 68), and the only building left from that period. The Marrakech Museum (see page 83) has a delightful outdoor café to enjoy a coffee, or perhaps another mint tea. Alternatively, head towards the nearest taxi for a ride up to the Le Jardin Majorelle (Majorelle Gardens, see page 98). Spend the evening at the Jemaa el Fna, listening to the (Arabic) storytellers and musicians.

2–3 DAYS: TIME TO SEE MUCH MORE

Take advantage of the extra time to visit some more sights, such as El Badi Palace ruins (see page 73) and the Saadian Tombs (see page 80).

With a day or two more, it's possible to view some museums, including the Dar Si Said's assembly of fine Moroccan decorative art (see page 81), or Dar Tiskiwin (see page 82), holding the private stash of the Dutch art collector Bert Flint. Sit back in the seat of a horse-drawn calèche while circling the city walls. Shop up and down rue de la Liberté in Guéliz. Spend an afternoon in the hammam, and enjoy the attentions of a professional scrubber, as well as a massage.

LONGER: ENJOYING MARRAKECH TO THE FULL

If it's possible to get away from browsing and shopping in the souks, or watching the continually changing entertainment at the Jemaa, a day or more away from the city shows off an entirely different side of Morocco. There are numerous possibilities for excursions into the High Atlas Mountains (see page 114), ranging from visiting a truly rural weekly market, to ascending the tallest mountain in North Africa. Another option for a few days is to head towards the seaside, particularly the charming and laid-back fishing village of Essaouira (see page 126). With its long, wide beach and excellent windsurfing environment, but without the development and tourism of Agadir, this artists' haven is a delightful break from the energy of Marrakech.

● *Make time for a cup of mint tea during your visit*

Something for nothing

Marrakech is not an expensive city and most entry fees to museums are pretty low. Nevertheless, if looking after every single dirham is an issue, then there are several options for free things to do.

Most interesting is the entertainment in the Jemaa el Fna, for which there is no charge. Of course, the performers work for tips, but these are not mandatory. Storytellers, who don't speak in French or English anyway, will begin their tales and stop when

○ *They don't charge, but musicians in the Medina will expect a tip*

they reach a critical point. Here, they will ask for an onlooker to give some money to continue, and generally someone does. Musicians and dancers work the crowd and all are invited to watch. It's possible to have a fascinating afternoon or evening without spending a penny.

Further within the Medina are the souks that seem to extend endlessly. When the markets appear to come to an end, they start again a bit further on, so that 'window shopping' is an activity that can easily take all day. Sometimes it's possible to witness craftsmen making their goods, seeing how wool is dyed in the Souk Sebbaghine, or watching leather goods being stitched in the Souk Cherratine.

The gardens outside the city walls are open to the public at no charge, and are well attended. The Koutoubia Gardens (see page 75) have roses for most of the year and are pleasant to walk through, although sometimes a little unkempt. A little further along is the Cyber Parc (see page 149), lovely well-manicured gardens dotted with computer terminals allowing you to go online pretty cheaply. The bright Moroccan sunshine often means it's difficult to see the screen, but the locals seem to use the machines in any weather. The other well-known green spaces are a bit further away, and require either quite a long walk or a short taxi ride. The historic Ménara Gardens (see page 98) have a large pond with a famous pavilion on their edge. A bit characterless, this place is best outside of the summer, when the air is clear and the often snow-covered Atlas Mountains are reflected in the water. The Agdal Gardens are open on Fridays and Sundays. Locals love to take along their stale bread and feed the ravenous – and increasingly large and insatiable – carp in the reservoir.

When it rains

Wet weather can turn unpaved roads into muddy slush and slow traffic down. It's not usually a problem, though, as rain falls mostly in the winter, and even then, the average is barely more than a couple of centimetres per month. Unfortunately, it tends to come down all at once, so it's probably wise to hide out if the sky begins to turn dark grey.

The best places to take refuge while still enjoying the sights are the museums. The Dar Si Said (see page 81) in the Medina is in a beautifully preserved palace, and comprises the South Morocco Regional Arts Museum. A quick dash away is the Dar Tiskiwin (see page 82) and the contents, Moroccan traditional art, are inside the house of the owner. Not far away is the Lazama Synagogue, and it's possible to visit it in the rain, although by the time you find your way there, through the twists and turns of the Jewish Mellah (see page 75), you might already be soaked (it's best to request directions from a local and accept that, by asking, you're hiring an unofficial guide). Further north is the Marrakech Museum (see page 83), a large rambling palace that has lots of rooms and various permanent and visiting exhibitions. If the rain isn't too bad, it might be worth taking in the Ben Youssef Medersa (see page 70) nearby, as much of it is covered. Some of the private galleries such as La Qoubba Galerie d'Art (see page 87) in the Medina, or the Matisse Art Gallery (see page 101) in Guéliz, have the work of contemporary Moroccan artists, which makes a change from seeing all that 'old stuff'.

Bad weather might provide an excellent chance to try the hammams (see page 41) located at various places throughout the city, and available in all shapes and sizes (and prices): wallowing in a bathhouse is a very Moroccan thing to do. Add a massage to complete the experience.

Alternatively, you might want to take in a film. The Mégarama Theatre's nine screens will offer a variety of choices (see page 112). Check to see whether your film of choice has subtitles or is dubbed before heading in that direction.

Having a cup of coffee, or sipping yet another mint tea, can also be a way of taking shelter on a wet day. Even some of the more basic cafés, such as those surrounding the Jemaa el Fna, give some sort of cover, while providing an opportunity for some great people-watching.

⬤ *It doesn't rain often but when it does, head for a hammam*

On arrival

TIME DIFFERENCE

Morocco is on Greenwich Mean Time. Daylight saving time was introduced in 2008. Clocks go forward one hour at the beginning of June and fall back one hour around the 20 August. Daylight saving dates are liable to change, so contact the tourist office to check.

ARRIVING

The most convenient way to get to Marrakech for a short break is to fly. Planes land at Marrakech Menara Airport, very close to the city centre. With a bit more time, travelling by train is an option, and although only domestic routes travel through Morocco, it's possible to make the relevant connection for the south just after the ferry port, at Tangier. As for driving, the fastest way from Europe is to cross the Straits of Gibraltar, head west towards Casablanca then south to Marrakech.

By air

Marrakech Menara Airport (☎ 05 24 44 79 10), is a mere 6 km (4 miles) west of the city centre. The airport is small but well renovated, and contains a few shops and a small restaurant as well as a bureau de change. To get into the city, catch the inexpensive local bus no. 11 from just outside the terminal building. It runs every 20 minutes during the week, or at slightly longer intervals at the weekend, to Jemaa el Fna. Alternatively, take a taxi and agree on a price before leaving the airport. A ride in a petit taxi (see page 65) should cost around 50 dirham but will only take three passengers. A grand taxi takes six passengers and costs around 100 dirham.

By rail

Marrakech's shiny new **railway station** (🄰 Corner av. Hassan II & Mohammed VI 🄾 08 90 20 30 40) was opened in 2009, right near the charming former railway building in Guéliz. The central hall is filled with natural light and there are plenty of shops and restaurants. You can travel to most destinations in Morocco from here, and it's advisable to travel first class if possible. See the ONCF website 🆆 www.oncf.ma for timetables and information.

By road

Long-distance buses are by far the least expensive way to travel across

◗ Taxis are a convenient way to get around the city

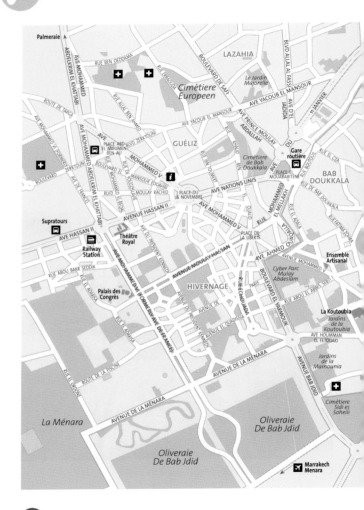

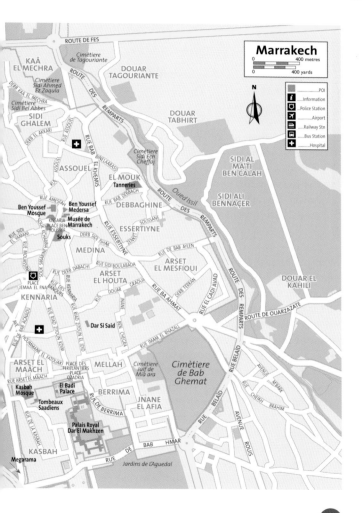

IF YOU GET LOST, TRY …

Excuse me, is this the right way to the tourist office/ the bus station?
Excusez-moi, c'est la bonne direction pour l'office de tourisme/la gare routière?
Ekskewzaymwah, seh lah bon deerekseeawng poor lohfeece de tooreezm/lah gahr rootyair?

Can you point to it on my map?
Pouvez-vous me le montrer sur la carte?
Poovehvoo mer ler mawngtreh sewr lah kart?

Morocco, although they take much longer than planes or trains. For destinations close to Marrakech, such as Essaouira, they are a cheaper option than taxis.

The main **gare routière** (bus station ❸ pl. el Mouarabitène, Bab Doukkala ☎ 05 24 43 39 33) can be a bit chaotic. The Guéliz departure point may be a bit easier to handle (❸ 12 blvd Zerktouni ☎ 05 24 44 83 28). Although driving within the city is neither necessary nor recommended, it can be useful to have a car when exploring the rest of Morocco. A toll motorway links Tangier, Rabat, Casablanca and Marrakech, and a new motorway to Agadir is under construction. If staying in the Medina, take your chances and leave the car in a car park, near the city wall. Note that people tending car parks will often ask that you leave the keys, so they can move the car if required, as lots are often parked in tightly. Alternatively, choose a hotel that has a large parking area, such as in Guéliz or the Palmeraie.

● *Hitting the bustling streets of Marrakech may bring on culture shock*

FINDING YOUR FEET

Overall, Marrakech is pretty safe, adhering to the rules of respect inherent in Muslim tradition. Nevertheless, crime is increasing in the Medina so keep an eye on valuables and don't walk alone after 22.00. It's also advisable to dress respectfully, especially for women. Keep shoulders covered, and wear trousers or long skirts, rather than shorts, at least in the Medina.

ORIENTATION

A huge ochre wall surrounds the historic centre completely and is a useful way of recognising the line between the old (Medina, basically) and new areas of the city, which are Guéliz, Hivernage and the surrounding areas. The focal point of the Medina is the main square, the Jemaa el Fna, which is directly across from the Koutoubia, the tall minaret that is visible from almost any open space. If lost, just ask for the Jemaa, and most people will be able to offer directions. The souk area is to the north of the main square.

To the south are some of the most important attractions, and past the Badi is the Royal Palace. On the extended grounds of this regal residence are the Agdal Gardens. The Medina is surrounded by intact walls, and there are various gates, known as *babs*, through which to enter, some wide enough for cars and others for foot traffic only. Some of the bigger roads around the edges can support motor vehicles but, in general, the Medina is a pedestrian area. Horse-drawn calèches, motor scooters, donkey carts and bicycles are exceptions, but that doesn't mean there is actually enough room – watch out for them when wandering through some of the major thoroughfares.

To the west of the Jemaa, outside the city walls, is the Hivernage area and southern side of Guéliz. Avenue Mohammed V straddles the division between the two sections of the city, and goes past place du 16 Novembre to place Abd el Moumen Ben Ali (see page 96), the heart of the large modern city with its wide boulevards and heavy traffic.

GETTING AROUND

There are no metro or tram systems in Marrakech. One good option, if you want to see a lot of sights without wearing out too much shoe leather, is the **hop-on, hop-off bus** (☎ 05 25 06 00 06 ⓦ www.city-sightseeing.com). You can purchase a ticket for either 24 or 48 hours and get on and off as many times as you like. The bus even travels out to Palmeraie. A more romantic option is to hire a horse-drawn calèche – there are many patrolling the city's main tourist areas.

Visiting the Medina is best done on foot, although you can reach some areas by taxi. Taxis are a pale yellow colour and can be shared *grand* (large) or individual *petit* (small) cabs. If you're in a small

SPELLING MATTERS

You may find that the spelling of street and place names varies wildly in Morocco. For example, Marrakech is sometimes spelled 'Marrakesh' with an 'sh'. The town of Essaouira can be spelled 'Essouira' on some maps. Neither spelling is officially correct or incorrect. In most of the Medina's many neighbourhoods there is a street named 'Caid' or 'Kaid', which is roughly equivalent to 'High street'. To make matters more confusing, some street names start with the French *rue* and others start with the Moroccan *derb*. At least it's fun to get lost!

group it's cheaper to take a petit taxi, but prices are reasonable either way. Petit taxis cannot travel beyond the city limits.

There are usually meters, but drivers are often hesitant to use them so it's best to agree on a price beforehand. Daytime journeys within the city shouldn't be much more than 60–70 dirham, but prices do go up after 21.00. If you intend to visit a specific destination outside the city, ask at your hotel for advice on an appropriate price.

CAR HIRE

There is no need to have your own transport for a city break in Marrakech. Even for short excursions to destinations nearby, hiring a taxi for a day or two is probably cheaper than renting a car. If you are planning an extended visit to places further away, hiring a vehicle is an option, although it's relatively expensive to do so. It's best to stick with the larger, better-known rental companies, as they are more reliable, and their insurance coverage guaranteed. Better deals might be found by booking a car as part of a fly-drive package.

Avis ℡ 05 24 43 31 69 🅦 www.avis.ma

Budget ℡ Airport: 05 24 43 88 75; Guéliz: 05 42 43 11 80
🅦 www.budget.com

Europcar ℡ 022 31 37 37 🅦 www.1stmaroc.com/europcar

Hertz ℡ Airport: 05 24 44 72 30; Guéliz: 05 24 43 99 84
🅦 www.hertz.co.uk

Thrifty ℡ 06 61 80 69 63

❿ *This is just one of the areas where you can find great places to eat*

THE CITY OF
Marrakech

The Old City: the Medina

Many of Marrakech's tourist attractions are located within the Medina. Surrounded by walls that are worth a look in their own right, the ancient city contains the Jemaa el Fna (the central square, see page 73), monuments, mosques, museums, palaces and tombs that are what visitors come to see. The souks, the typical markets, seem to go on endlessly with their phenomenal array of goods, and are probably the best in North Africa. Street cafés are everywhere, and sipping mint tea or coffee in an open square or exclusive private *riad* is a great way to take a break. There are restaurants ranging from casual locales to fine gourmet venues with excellent views. Beginning at dusk, the Jemaa has dozens of stalls where food is selected, prepared and served right in front of its customers. The main square is where the majority of the Medina's entertainment is based, during both day and night.

SIGHTS & ATTRACTIONS

Almoravid Qoubba

This unassuming domed ablutions pool is the only structure left from the period of the Almoravids (early 12th century). Unimpressive from a distance, once inside, the ancient fountain is simple yet nicely decorated. ❸ pl. Ben Youssef, Kissaria ⏱ 09.00–16.00

La Bahia Palace

Hidden behind high walls that insulate the grounds from noise, as well as the outside world, this magnificent palace was the residence of Ba Ahmed Ben Moussa, a grand vizier in the 19th century. Built for his four wives, 24 concubines and their brood, the complex

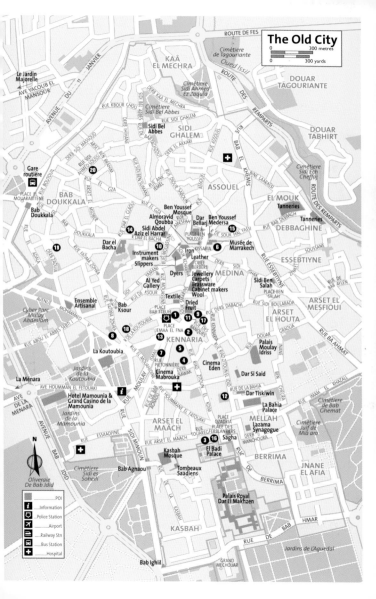

The Old City

| 0 | 300 metres |
| 0 | 300 yards |

ROUTE DE FES

Cimetière de Tagouriante

Oued Issil

DOUAR TAGOURIANTE

KAÂ EL MECHRA

Le Jardin Majorelle

AVE YACOUB EL MANSOUR

AVENUE DU 11 JANVIER

Cimetière Sidi Ahmed Ez Zaquia

Cimetière Sidi Bel Abbes

DOUAR TABHIRT

Cimetière Sidi Ech Cheffaj

ROUTE DES REMPARTS

SIDI GHALEM

Sidi Bel Abbes

BAB EL KHEMIS

Gare routière

BAB DOUKKALA

ASSOUEL

EL MOUK

Tanneries

Bab Doukkala

PLACE MOUARABTIENNE

Tanneries

DEBBAGHINE

Ben Youssef Mosque

Almoravid Qoubba

Dar Bellarj

Ben Youssef Medersa

Musée de Marrakech

ESSEBTIYNE

Sidi Abdel Aziz el Harrar

Dar el Bacha

Instrument makers

Slippers

Iron

Leather

Sidi Ben Salah

PLACE BEN YOUSSEF

KISSARIA

MEDINA

ARSET EL MESFIOUI

Ensemble Artisanal

Al Yed Gallery

Bab Ksour

Dyers

Textile

Jewellery Carpets Brassware Cabinet makers Wool

ARSET EL HOUTA

Dried Fruit

Palais Moulay Idriss

La Koutoubia

PLACE BAB FTEUH

PLACE JEMAA EL FNA

KENNARIA

Cinema Eden

Dar Si Said

La Koutoubia

Cinema Mabrouka

Dar Tiskiwin

Hotel Mamounia & Grand Casino de la Mamounia

La Bahia Palace

Jardins de la Koutoubia

Jardins de la Mamounia

MELLAH

Lazama Synagogue

La Ménara

ARSET EL MAÂCH

Sagha

BERRIMA

AVENUE DE LA MENARA

Kasbah Mosque

El Badi Palace

JNANE EL AFIA

Oliveraie De Bab Jdid

Cimetière Sidi es Soheïli

Bab Agnaou

Tombeaux Saadiens

Palais Royal Dar El Makhzen

KASBAH

Bab Ighlil

GRAND MECHOUAR

Jardins de L'Aguedal

Legend

POI

- i Information
- Police Station
- Airport
- Railway Stn
- Bus Station
- Hospital

is a sequence of courtyards, fountains and chambers. Exquisitely
enhanced with painted ceilings, fine stucco detailing and carved
wood, the palace presents excellent examples of period interior
decoration and is a delightful place to linger. ⓐ rue Riad Zitoun el
Jdid ① 05 24 38 97 79 ① 08.00–11.45, 14.45–17.45. Admission charge

Ben Youssef Medersa

Built as a Koranic school in the 16th century, the Medersa is a series
of simple, monastic-like student rooms surrounding a large central
courtyard. The pool in the centre is made from Carrara marble, which
glows white in the bright sunshine. The common areas, like the prayer
rooms and classrooms, are magnificently decorated with incredibly
elaborate carvings in stucco and wood. A stunning example of
Moorish architecture and design. ⓐ pl. Ben Youssef, Kissaria
① 05 24 44 18 93 ① 09.00–19.00

City Gates (Babs)

Puncturing the relatively featureless walls are the 19 city gates.
Located all around the Medina, some of these entrances are
magnificent gateways while others are simply modern access
points. Bab Agnaou and the Royal Palace's Bab Ighlil to the south
are two of the more impressive portals.

City Walls

Enclosing the Medina, these 10 m (33 ft) high walls follow the
original 12th-century ramparts built by the Sultan Ali Ben Youssef.
Still constructed from *pisé* (mud and clay mixed with straw and
lime), they run the 10 km (6 mile) circumference around the old city.

● *The Medersa is a stunning example of detailed Moorish architecture*

A WALK IN THE MEDINA – PALACES

Begin at the Jemaa el Fna with the Koutoubia mosque behind you. Cross the square, then turn right into the rue Riad Zitoun el Kdim. Follow this bigger street south to place Qzadria. En route, wander into the side passages, getting a glimpse into some of Marrakech's real life. Seemingly confusing, the little streets will eventually take the pedestrian to a larger thoroughfare that leads to the square. Don't be afraid to get lost – all routes eventually get through and the locals can always give directions to the major tourist sites. On arrival, cross over to place des Ferblantiers and take a look at the beautiful lamps, candelabra and other items crafted in metal. Opposite the square is the treasure chest of the Sagha, the small arcade stuffed full of gold jewellery stores. Place Qzadria is a good central location. Heading east will lead to the beautiful 19th-century Bahia Palace. Across from here is the Mellah, the Jewish quarter, in which is located the old synagogue. More confusing to explore than it appears on maps, ask the locals for help if you get lost. Immediately south of place Qzadria are the impressive remains of El Badi Palace. Continuing in the same direction leads to the Royal Palace, and the Agdal Gardens beyond.

Back to the square, head west to the entryway of the Kasbah. Turn left alongside the city walls, then left again near the enormous Bab Agnaou city gate, to take you past the magnificent Kasbah mosque. Just beyond is the entrance to the Saadian Tombs. Retrace your steps to get back to the Jemaa.

The best way to view their entirety is by horse-drawn calèche, as on the route are areas of not much interest to the pedestrian. The stretch at the Medina entrance leading from the Avenue de la Menara is particularly dramatic.

El Badi Palace

The large ruins of El Badi still give off an aura of wealth and power. Once 'incomparable', the lavish 16th-century palace of Ahmed El Mansour was so legendary that the subsequent Alaouite dynasty's Sultan Moulay Ismail took a full ten years to strip it of its luxurious materials. Today, it's quite peaceful strolling around the vast concrete grounds with what remains of the walls. From the upper levels there is a spectacular view of the High Atlas Mountains on clear days. On display in the exhibition area in the back is the 17th-century wooden *minbar* (pulpit) taken from the Koutoubia.

The storks resting on their gigantic nests, perched on the corners of the top floors, are also fun to watch. The open-air Badi Palace often hosts major events, including the Festival of Popular Arts in July and the International Film Festival (see page 14) in November.
ⓐ pl. des Ferblantiers, Berrima 🕐 08.00–11.45, 14.45–17.45. Admission charge

Jemaa el Fna

This large open space is the Medina's centre, in spirit rather than in geography. Everything leads back to this square and it's always a handy reference point. Jeema el Fna comes alive at night with traditional Moroccan entertainment (see page 36). It lies next to the Koutoubia minaret and alongside Mohammed V, the major urban thoroughfare of Marrakech.

Kasbah

This area of the Medina is the most complete urban Kasbah (defined as the citadel, or quarter in which the citadel is located) in Morocco. It was built in the 12th century to house the servants and employees attendant to the Almohad Royal Palace, once located just to the south. The construction extended the city boundaries. One of the most impressive gates in the original wall, the Bab Agnaou, is the entryway through which one enters the Kasbah. Dominated by the beautiful minaret of the Kasbah mosque, the enclave has a 'city within a city' feel. The Saadian Tombs are located here.

La Koutoubia

Marrakech's icon is the minaret of the Koutoubia ('booksellers') mosque, named after the businesses that once thrived at its base. Built in the 12th century in a Hispano-Moorish style similar to its cousin, the Giralda in Seville, its dimensions of 1:5, width to height, make the tower slim and graceful. The mosque to which the Koutoubia belongs is not accessible to non-Muslims, but the square next to it, and the adjoining rose gardens, are open to the public. ⓐ rue de la Koutoubia

Mellah

The Jewish quarter of the Medina is a ghost of what it used to be, as most of the members of the once-large Jewish population left in the mid- to late 20th century. The narrow winding streets are run-down and of little interest to tourists.

Within the district remains the ancient Lazama Synagogue. Originally constructed in the 16th century when the Jews were an important part of the commercial life of the Medina, it's now the

◀ *The minaret of a mosque – La Koutoubia – forms the city's landmark* oldest one left in the city. If you can find your way there, tours are offered by the resident custodian. A large but unimpressive Jewish cemetery lies to the east.

Also in the Mellah is a small, unassuming covered market selling spices and basics. Nearby is the Sagha, the Marché des Bijouterie, or gold market. Located discreetly within a small arcade, the shop windows are stuffed full of gold trinkets. **Lazama Synagogue** ⓐ Derb Manchoura ⓛ 09.00–18.00

Mosques

Even though Marrakech's mosques are not open to non-Muslims, the buildings are still an important part of the cityscape. The exteriors are dramatic and often quite beautiful, with the tall minarets not only typical examples of period architecture, but also excellent landmarks by which to find your way through the Medina. The call to prayer, broadcast five times a day, gets to be a familiar sound.

A few of the more outstanding mosques are:

Bab Doukkala ⓐ rue de Bab Doukkala
Ben Youssef ⓐ near the Medersa at pl. Ben Youssef, Kissaria
Kasbah ⓐ rue de la Kasbah
La Koutoubia ⓐ rue de la Koutoubia

Souks

Defined as Arabic or North African markets, Marrakech's souks are stalls and shops that sell a huge range of crafts, food and general goods. Located predominately to the north of the Jemaa, there are so many of these stalls running into each other that this entire area of the Medina seems to be one gigantic street market. Divided approximately according to the area of speciality, it's possible to navigate through this shopping maze based on the sorts of items

⬤ *In their traditional garb, water sellers hawk their wares on the Jemaa el Fna*

⬤ *Souks are crammed with stalls that specialise in particular products*

visible. Narrow thoroughfares sell goods that relate to the main features on the larger routes, although some of these hideaways have their own sub-specialities. Usually under the cover of a slatted roof that lets in shafts of light, and so loaded with items that each stall seems to be overflowing, the souks can be crowded, especially at peak times. Shopping at quieter periods might be easier. Bargaining is the way to go, with virtually no stallholder giving his true lowest price at first request (see Bargaining, page 26).

Squares

Every so often, the cramped and crowded streets of the Medina give way to a spacious open area. Often, the square, or *place*, is worth attention in itself. Some of the more notable ones are:

A WALK IN THE MEDINA – SOUKS

Walking away from the Koutoubia across the Jemaa el Fna, turn left into any of the passageways crowded with goods. The souks begin here, and it's best to wander at will, the decision to turn left and right depending on what attracts the eye. At first overwhelming, it soon becomes apparent that the different souks specialise, and that it's possible to orient oneself depending on the type of item that's for sale.

Meandering more or less north, one comes eventually to the place Ben Youssef, a less claustrophobic open square around which are located three of the Medina's major sights: the Ben Youssef Medersa, the Almoravid Qoubba and the Marrakech Museum. Head south again, choosing other passageways and different souks, to find your way back to the Jemaa.

Ben Youssef (located in Kissaria) More or less off this square are located three of Marrakech's most important sites, the Ben Youssef Medersa, the Almoravid Qoubba and the Marrakech Museum

Criée Berbère Emerging from the depths of the souk, here is where the carpet merchants show off their brightly coloured wares

Ferblantiers In this very central location are the tinsmiths, producing all kinds of candleholders, lanterns and light fixtures

Grand Mechouar This broad open space to the south of the Medina was attached to the Royal Palace, and once served as a waiting room

Jemaa el Fna The most important square in Marrakech (see page 73)

Qzadria A pleasant park with benches and shade, this green space is a good place from which to navigate around the southern Medina

Tombeaux Saadiens (Saadian Tombs)

Hidden away under the shadow of the Kasbah mosque is
a discreet entrance that leads through a series of passages.
At the end is a large garden, with open rooms, elaborate mosaics
and finely carved wood. At various places throughout the complex,
raised slightly above the ground, are elongated slabs. These markers
are the tombs of the Saadians, the dynasty that held power from
the mid-16th to mid-17th century. Hidden and forgotten until
the 1920s, their rediscovery unearthed one of the nicest sites
in Marrakech, with cool gardens, fine artwork and a generally
tranquil atmosphere. ➌ rue de la Kasbah, Bab Agnaou
🕐 08.00–11.45, 14.00–17.45

STORYTELLERS OF THE JEMAA

The storytellers of Marrakech's main square, the Jemaa el Fna,
are one of the main reasons that UNESCO has designated this
area as a humanity heritage site. Important exponents of the
oral tradition, these tellers of tales always manage to gather
huge crowds around them. Speaking in Arabic, they cater their
accounts to locals rather than tourists. The storyteller begins
his tale, building up the tension – and just as he comes to
a critical point, stops. At this stage, the speaker will ask the
audience if anyone is willing to pay him to continue. Inevitably,
someone rises from the group, hands the teller a coin, and
the man continues with his story. As the evening progresses,
so does the tale, with the listeners eventually getting the
whole account, and the storyteller earning his keep.

Zaouias

Marrakech is an Islamic holy city, and still a pilgrimage destination, due to it being the final resting place of The Seven Saints. Living between the 12th and 16th centuries, the holies were: Sidi Cadi Ayad, Sidi As-Soheyli, Sidi Yousef Bin Ali, Sidi Bel Abbis, Sidi Bin Sliman Al Jazouli, Sidi Abdal Aziz Tebba and Sidi Al Ghazwani. The tomb of a *marabout*, or holy person, when it becomes the central focus of a mosque, is known as a *zaouia*. Although not open to non-Muslims, it's worth understanding the significance of these places when attempting a peek inside the mosque.

Some of the more important *zaouias* are **Sidi Abdel Aziz el Harrar** (ⓐ rue Mouassine), **Sidi Bel Abbes** (ⓐ rue de Bab Taghzout) and **Sidi Ben Salah** (ⓐ pl. Ben Salah).

CULTURE

Most of the Medina's culture is visible on the streets, in its architecture, crafts and performances. There are few formal museums.

Dar Bellarj

Once a hospital for injured storks, this *riad* is now the Foundation for Moroccan Culture. Exhibitions on all aspects of national arts are held here. ⓐ 9 rue Toualot Zaouiat Lakhdar, north of entrance to Ben Youssef Medersa ☎ 05 24 44 45 55 ⏰ 09.00–13.00, 14.00–18.30

Dar Si Said

Located in a lavish palace, this assembly is also known as the South Morocco Regional Arts Museum. The collections include Berber jewellery, cedar-wood furniture, carpets, and window and door frames. ⓐ rue Riad Zitoun el Jdid ☎ 05 24 38 95 64 🕔 09.00–11.45, 15.00–17.45 Sat–Thur, 09.00–11.30, 15.00–17.45 Fri

Dar Tiskiwin

Bert Flint, a Dutch art historian, exhibits his personal collection of traditional Moroccan art objects within his own charming

NAMES OF THE SOUKS

The following is a list of some of Marrakech's souks, with the Arabic, and where they vary, French, names:

English	Arabic	French
Metalwork	**Attarine**	
Cabinet makers	**Chouari**	*Ebenistes*
Carpets	**Zarbia**	*Tapis*
Dried fruit, nuts, etc	**Kchacha**	
Dyers	**Sebbaghine**	*Teinturier*
Instrument makers	**Kimakhine**	*des Musiciens*
Iron	**Haddadine**	*Fer*
Jewellery		*Bijoutiers*
Leather	**El Kebir**	*Cuir*
Saddlers	**Serrajine**	
Slippers	**Smata**	*Babouches*
Spices	**Kassabine**	*Épices*
Tanners	**Cherratine**	*Tanneurs*
Textiles	**Smarine**	*Textiles*
Traditional medicine	**Kedima**	*Apothecaries*
Wool	**Laghzal**	*Laine*

Hispano-Moorish style home. ⓐ 8 rue de la Bahia, rue Riad Zitoun el Jdid ⓣ 05 24 38 91 92 ⓛ 10.00–12.30, 15.00–17.30

Ensemble Artisanal

Although primarily a series of shops, this complex is also an area of workshops for craftsmen. It's possible to watch artisans creating their specialist items in situ, without worrying about being hassled to buy. Prices are fixed and function as a good guide to how much items in the souks should cost. ⓐ av. Mohammed V ⓣ 05 24 42 38 35 ⓛ 08.00–19.30

Musée de Marrakech (Marrakech Museum)

Previously a fabulous 19th-century palace, the building has now been converted to a large museum. Although changing exhibitions feature various aspects of traditional craft, the palace itself is what makes the visit worthwhile. ⓐ pl. Ben Youssef, Kissaria ⓣ 05 24 39 09 11 ⓛ 09.00–18.30

RETAIL THERAPY

Fruit, vegetable and fish markets spring up at will all over the Medina. The main shopping area is just north of the Jemaa el Fna. Most shops are open 09.00–18.00 every day, and sometimes later in the souks. Lunch breaks, usually from 13.00–15.00, are not uncommon.

Al Yed Gallery Specialising in antique Berber jewellery, the shop also has an excellent collection of ceramics from the 12th to 19th centuries. ⓐ 66 rue Fhal Chidmi, off rue Mouassine ⓣ 05 24 44 29 95

L'Art de Taznakhte: Chez Brahim Kilims are the speciality here, as well as wonderful old poufs made from Moroccan blankets. 🅰 Carpets souk 🕐 05 24 44 01 10 🕐 09.00–19.00

Artisan Souffletier Unique gifts for friends who have fireplaces, or even for those who don't, these bellows are artisan-crafted and detailed in various different materials, including wood, leather and metal. 🅰 10 Ensemble Artisanal, av. Mohammed V 🕐 08.00–13.00, 14.00–19.00

Arts de Marrakech Just one of many carpet stalls in Marrakech, but you are certain of getting a good bargain here – if you negotiate hard enough! 🅰 85 pl. Rahba Kdima (Carpets souk) 🕐 05 24 44 53 85 🕐 08.00–20.00

Beldi Hidden among the indistinguishable stalls in the souk, this little shop sells the finest – and most expensive – traditional Moroccan clothing. Prices are non-negotiable! 🅰 9–11 Souikat Laksour, near place Bab Fteuh 🕐 05 24 44 10 76 🕐 09.00–13.00, 16.00–19.30

Bellawi Abdellatif Antique clothing and Berber marriage belts are some of the things carried by this shop. More whimsical items like the pom-pom hats worn by the water sellers in the Jemaa are also on sale. 🅰 56 Kissaria Alousta (Leather souk) 🕐 06 59 97 13 39 🕐 09.00–19.30

Complexe d'Artisanat This large storehouse of Moroccan goods is adequate for shoppers who don't enjoy the intimacy (or claustrophobia)

CARPETS AND KILIMS

Whether in the Medina or travelling outside the city of Marrakech, it is hard to avoid these typical Moroccan craftwares. Both of these types of floor coverings are produced by traditional methods of weaving, although their forms are different.

A Moroccan carpet is a pile rug, which is knotted. The pile threads form the front and can be thick and heavy, with either a longer or shorter tuft. High Atlas rugs are quite soft with simple, graphic designs produced in a wide range of colours.

A kilim (or *hanbal*) is a rug that's flat woven, with the threads on the underside. Used more for hangings, covers and saddlebags, they are made by nomadic and semi-nomadic tribes often in very complex geometric patterns.

of the souk area but still want a wide selection of items. Located in the Kasbah district, far away from the rabble. ⓐ 7 Derb Baissi, rue de la Kasbah ⓣ 05 24 38 18 53 ⓛ 09.00–19.30

El Abidi Nasser Eddine This little store has exquisite Berber jewellery. Unlike most of the souks, prices here are fixed. ⓐ 9 rue Smarine (Jewellery souk) ⓣ 06 66 11 14 72 ⓛ 09.00–20.30

FNAC A branch of the large chain of stores that started in France, the stall sells books and batteries. In 1941, this corner shop was the first bookshop in Marrakech. ⓐ 64 Souikat Laksour, near place Bab Fteuh ⓣ 05 24 44 34 17 ⓛ 09.00–20.00

● *Colourful Moroccan slippers known as* babouches *are in the Medina's souks*

Herboristerie Malih This spice market near the Mellah's smaller *bab* has an excellent selection of herbs, spices and alternative medicines.
ⓐ 184 Hay Essalame, off rue Riad Zitoun el Jdid, Mellah ☎ 05 24 38 74 03

KifKif Pretty and unusual items for the home, with colourful small tassels and pom-poms adorning linens and towels.

A perfect stop if you need to buy gifts. 🅐 8 rue de Ksour, near Bab Ksour 🅣 06 61 08 20 41 🆆 www.kifkifbystef.com

La Maison de Caftan Marocain (The House of the Moroccan Caftan) A huge collection of fabulous Moroccan clothing of the highest quality is available here. This shop is also known for its famous clientele, with customers including Jean-Paul Gaultier and the late Alan Bates. 🅐 65 rue Sidi el Yamani, off rue Mouassine 🅣 05 24 44 10 51 🅛 08.00–20.00

Le Monde de la Poupée (The World of the Doll) The artisan resident in the shop creates dolls made of fabric and dressed in traditional Moroccan style. Something a bit different from the usual souvenirs! 🅐 114 Kissaria Hadj Abdeslam, near pl. Ben Youssef 🅣 05 24 44 10 49 🅛 09.00–20.30 summer; 09.00–19.00 winter

No. 67, Souk Teinturier Well-crafted lanterns and other copper objects are on offer in this little shop. 🅐 67 Souk Teinturier (Dyers' Souk) 🅣 06 62 83 81 11

Original Design Wedged among the tinsmiths is this ceramics store, featuring finely made work in contemporary colours. 🅐 47 pl. des Ferblantiers 🅣 05 24 38 03 61 🅛 09.00–19.00

Ouamhane Although all sorts of wooden items are found here, the shop specialises in games, such as backgammon and solitaire. 🅐 27-29 Souk Laghzal (Wool Souk) 🅣 06 10 51 03 76 🅛 09.00–19.00

La Qoubba Galerie d'Art A venue for displaying both new and established Moroccan artists, this gallery is one of the better-

known places to pick up some contemporary art. ⓐ 91 Souk Talaa, near pl. Ben Youssef ① 05 24 38 05 15 ② 08.00–20.00 ⓦ www.art-gallery-marrakech.com

Warda La Mouche Lovely and wearable interpretations of Moroccan clothing for women. The tunics are especially coveted by Marrakchis. ⓐ 127 rue Kennaria, southeast of Jemaa el Fna ① 05 24 38 90 63 ② 09.00–19.30

TAKING A BREAK

Aqua £ ❶ With Italian owners, this little café, right on the Jemaa el Fna, has excellent small salads and homemade pastas. The small rooftop terrace gives you a view of all the action in the square. A scoop of one of the 15 flavours of *gelato* is perfect for taking away. ⓐ 68 pl. Jemaa el Fna ① 05 24 38 13 24 ② 07.00–00.00

Café de France £ ❷ The outside tables provide excellent vantage points of the square, and the breakfasts are pretty good, too. This is one of the landmark cafés in the Medina, and as almost everyone knows where it is, a great meeting point. ⓐ pl. Jemaa el Fna ① 05 24 44 23 19 ② 07.00–23.00

Café Palais el Badi £ ❸ On the upper terrace, this pleasant outdoor café is eye level with the storks of El Badi Palace. Stop for a light lunch or mint tea and look down at the action below. ⓐ 4 rue Touareg, Berrima ① 05 24 38 99 75 ② 09.00–23.00

◀ *Souks are just the place to find a useful souvenir of your visit*

Earth Café Marrakech £ ❹ Run by an Australian-Moroccan chef, this is the place to find 100 per cent vegetarian and vegan food, along with a range of freshly squeezed juices and herbal teas. Located in an old *riad* just a few steps from Jemaa el Fna, it's a great place to take a healthy break from the bustle of the shops and streets. ⓐ Derb Sawak, Riad Zitoun el Kdim ❶ 06 61 48 92 02 ⓦ www.earthcafemarrakech.com ❶ 11.00–late

Ice Legend £ ❺ On the corner of the Jemaa el Fna, this little place offers more than 40 homemade ice cream flavours and is a great way to beat the heat. No seating. ⓐ pl. Jemaa el Fna ❶ 05 24 44 42 00 ❶ 11.00–23.30

● *Café Arabe is a great place to kick back and relax over a drink*

Marrakech Museum Café £ ❻ In the front courtyard of this museum is a delightful, low-key spot to wind down and take a break. ❷ pl. Ben Youssef, Kissaria ● 09.00–18.00

Patisserie-salon de thé des Princes £ ❼ A huge selection of both Moroccan and Western pastries is available at this café, as well as ice cream. Sit inside, or take the goodies away. ❷ 32 rue de Bab Agnaou ● 05 24 44 30 33 ● 05.00–21.00

Portofino £ ❽ This Italian-owned restaurant offers the best pizza in town, and its air conditioning is a welcome relief in summer. Casual and perfect for the whole family. ❷ 279 av. Mohammed V ● 05 24 39 16 65 ● 12.00–23.00

Les Prémices £ ❾ One of the better offerings on the square, this French-managed café/restaurant is a good lunch spot, with salads, tagines, couscous, and more. Breakfast and snacks are served here, too. ❷ pl. Jemaa el Fna ● 05 24 39 19 70 ● 09.00–00.00

AFTER DARK

Café Arabe £ ❿ With beautiful décor, this Italian-owned renovated *riad* offers homemade pastas and other delicious fare. The bar on the top-floor terrace is stylish and the perfect place to while away the evening hours. ❷ 184 rue Mouassine ● 05 24 42 97 28 ● 11.00–00.00

Chez Chegrouni £ ⓫ This cheap and cheerful café on the Jemaa is the landing point for the petit taxis that can get no further into the Medina. Watch the characters while getting basic tagines and couscous. ❷ rue des Banques, off pl. Jemaa el Fna ● 07.00–23.00

Dar Mimouan £ ⑫ Good prices and ethnic cuisine are served in the courtyard of this old palace, even if the décor is a little over the top. ⓐ Derb Ben Amrane 1, rue Riad Zitoun el Jdid ① 05 24 44 33 48 ② 09.00–23.00

Jemaa el Fna £ ⑬ Eating at any of the stalls on the main square is an experience, and one way to select where to go is to see whose selection of food you like, as well as the number of locals huddled around the makeshift kitchens. ⓐ pl. Jemaa el Fna ② Dusk till around 22.00

Dar Moha ££ ⑭ Known for its nouvelle cuisine versions of Moroccan standards, the ambience of this fine restaurant is enhanced by its poolside location. ⓐ 81 rue Dar el Bacha ① 05 24 38 64 00 ⓦ www.darmoha.ma ② 12.00–15.00, 19.00–00.00 Tues–Sun

Fondouk ££ ⑮ Situated in the heart of the souks, this venue serves Moroccan cuisine but, unusually, blended with French Mediterranean flavouring – a nice change from the usual. ⓐ 55 rue de Souk Hal Fassi ① 05 24 37 81 90 ② 12.00–00.00

Kosybar ££ ⑯ A stylish restaurant for lunch and dinner and the only place to get good and reliable sushi in the Medina. The roof terrace offers a lovely view over a small, tree-filled square. ⓐ 47 pl. des Ferblantiers ① 05 24 38 03 24 ② 12.00–00.00

Le Marrakchi ££ ⑰ A fine restaurant that has one of the best views over the square and La Koutoubia beyond, especially at sunset. This place is highly recommended for a first-night dinner. ⓐ rue des Banques, off pl. Jemaa el Fna ① 05 24 44 33 77 ② 12.00–15.00, 19.00–22.30

● *The exquisite Dar Moha is both a visual and culinary treat*

Narwama ££ ⑱ Overshadowed by the high-profile Jardins de la Koutoubia Hotel, this predominantly Thai restaurant occupies a huge courtyard in one of the Medina's surprisingly large hidden locations. Makes a nice change from couscous! ⓐ 30 rue de la Koutoubia ⓣ 05 24 44 08 44 ⓛ 19.30–late

● *The stylish piano bar at Las Jardins de la Koutoubia*

Le Pavillon £££ ⑲ In this tastefully decorated *riad* lies, quite possibly, the best French restaurant in the city. Indulge in gastronomic fare including foie gras and bouillabaisse. Book in advance. ⓐ Derb Zaouia, Bab Doukkala ① 05 24 38 70 40 ① Dinner only, Wed–Mon

Le Yacout £££ ⑳ One of Marrakech's most exclusive restaurants is where the glitterati go when they want to be seen. The best of the best Moroccan food is served in this gorgeous 17th-century Arab residence. ⓐ 79 rue Sidi Ahmed Soussi ① 05 24 38 29 29 ① 20.00–23.30 (last seating 21.30)

BARS
Grand Hotel Tazi A little grubby, and right in the middle of things, this bar is one of the few places where you can get a beer in the old

town. A well-known backpackers' hotel and hang-out (see page 45), the cheap prices are very much appreciated by the clientele.
ⓐ Corner av. el Mouahidine & rue de Bab Agnaou, Medina
ⓣ 05 24 44 27 87 ⓛ 07.00–22.30

Piano Bar, Les Jardins de la Koutoubia Very upmarket, this comfortable place is located within a luxury hotel. It's a perfect spot for having a drink after watching the activities at the nearby Jemaa el Fna. ⓐ 26 rue de la Koutoubia ⓣ 05 24 38 88 00
ⓦ www.lesjardinsdelakoutoubia.com ⓛ 17.00–00.00

CASINO

Le Grand Casino de la Mamounia Technically just within the city walls, the Mamounia has a casino where you can bet away whatever cash you may have. The gambling area is very upmarket, and a dress code applies. ⓐ av. Bab Jdid, Medina ⓣ 05 24 44 45 70
ⓦ www.mamounia.com ⓛ 15.00–04.00 Mon–Fri, 14.00–04.00 Sat & Sun

CINEMAS

Cinema Eden Marrakech's oldest cinema invites locals and tourists alike to cram together in this little space, filled with folding chairs. The latest films are shown here, but they're just as likely to be Kung Fu movies as Hollywood blockbusters. ⓐ rue Riad Zitoun el Jdid, rue des Banques

Cinema Mabrouka This very popular venue right in the heart of the Medina's main pedestrianised street shows Bollywood, Hollywood and martial arts movies. ⓐ rue Pietonnière, rue de Bab Agnaou ⓣ 05 24 44 33 03

The New City: Guéliz, Hivernage, Sidi Ghanem & the Palmeraie

Soon after the Treaty of Fez was signed in 1912, which changed Morocco's status from an independent country to a colony of France, a town planner arrived to develop a new city in Marrakech alongside the old. The French section was deliberately arranged in an organised fashion, a complete contrast to the organic convolutions of the Medina. The modern city is less mysterious and exotic than the Medina, but it does hold some things of interest for the visitor. Le Jardin Majorelle (Majorelle Gardens, see page 98) are a prime attraction and upmarket shopping can certainly be found in the district. Far more bars, clubs and discos operate in the new city than in the Medina. The Hivernage area is home to many 4- and 5-star hotels, as well as numerous restaurants and clubs. Sidi Ghanem is the industrial part of town, but alongside the city's factories are a number of big showrooms, making this an interesting place to shop. The Palmeraie is a fashionable area of the city, known for its luxury hotels, golf courses and stables (see page 111).

SIGHTS & ATTRACTIONS

Abd El Moumen Ben Ali Square

The heart of Guéliz, this square is not an attraction in its own right, but it is important as the effective centre of the new city. Always busy, at the junction of the main Mohammed V and Mohammed Zerktouni boulevards, the area is noisy and full of life at any time of the day.

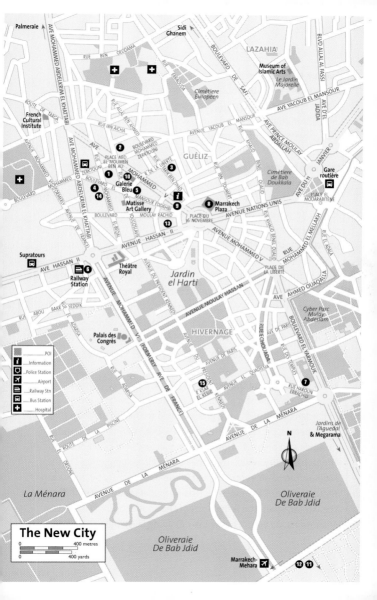

Avenue Mohammed V

Marrakech's main thoroughfare stretches from the northwestern corner of the Medina through Guéliz, passing some of the city's most important buildings along the way. It's worthwhile remembering this street for orientation.

Le Jardin Majorelle (Majorelle Gardens)

This magnificent collection of exotic plants, gathered around the bright blue former residence of its original owner, the artist Jacques Majorelle, is a wonderful respite in the new town. After Majorelle's death, the gardens started disintegrating and there was talk of using the grounds for urban development. In 1962, the fashion designer Yves Saint-Laurent and his partner, the artist Pierre Bergé, bought the park and brought it up to its current glorious condition. It's a pleasure to wander through this lush greenery made more striking by the occasional pot or detail in a bright, contrasting colour. The Museum of Islamic Arts (see page 102) now resides inside the main azure building. 📍 av. Yacoub el Mansour 📞 05 24 30 18 52 🌐 www.jardinmajorelle.com 🕐 08.00–18.30

La Ménara (Ménara Gardens)

At the far western end of the city are these 101 ha (250 acres) of gardens, filled with olive groves. Open to the public, people come here, especially on Fridays and Sundays, to stroll around the grounds and picnic. In the centre is a reservoir, in existence since the 12th century, which the Almohads built to supply water to the Medina. The pavilion, constructed in the 19th century by the sultan Moulay Abd er Rahman, is a pleasing visual focus, especially in the winter, when the reflections of the snow-covered High Atlas Mountains are visible in the lake. 📍 av. de la Ménara 🕐 05.00–18.30

● *The peace of the Majorelle Gardens contrasts with the bustle of life in the Medina*

Palais des Congrès

Typical of the new modern Moroccan architecture, this massive building is used for international meetings, as well as for conferences. In 1994, the Palais was the place where the GATT agreements were signed, establishing the World Trade Organization.

ⓐ av. Mohammed VI ① 05 24 33 91 00

Place du 16 Novembre

This centrally located square with its fountain is another good orientation point, even if the block architecture to the north is ugly.

🔺 *Marrakech's Théâtre Royal is the home of its opera and theatre*

To the southwest is the Jardin El Harti (Harti Gardens), simple and pleasant, with its alley of olive trees and a small playground for children.

Rue de la Liberté

In the heart of Guéliz, this small street has a disproportionate number of fine shops with goods ranging from gourmet pastries to elegant interior decoration. The avenue is a complete contrast to the souk experience, with no bartering allowed!

Théâtre Royal

In the Hivernage section of the new town, this impressive multifunctional arts complex is a striking landmark near the railway station. Built in a Moroccan-classical style with a row of palm trees alongside, the modern main building dominates the urban landscape. The auditorium puts on shows by the Théâtre Royal's in-house group, as well as being the venue for visiting theatre companies and the occasional conference. ❷ av. Mohammed VI ❶ 05 24 43 15 16 🕐 Box office: 08.00–12.00, 14.00–18.30

CULTURE

French Cultural Institute

This venue has a varying programme of cultural events, including dance, film and theatre events. The organisation features prominently during the International Film Festival (see page 14). ❷ route de Targa ❶ 05 24 44 69 30 Ⓦ www.ambafrance-ma.org

Matisse Art Gallery

Here is a gallery that displays the work of more interesting contemporary Moroccan artists, particularly those whose vision is a bit different from the usual. Items are for sale, but prices are high enough for the venue to function more as a display arena than a shop. ⓐ 61 rue Yougoslavie V ① 05 24 44 83 26 ⓦ www.matisse-art-gallery.com ① 10.00–13.00, 16.00–20.00 Tues–Sun

Museum of Islamic Arts in the Majorelle Gardens

Once the home of the gardens' eponymous artist-owner, the gorgeous blue house in the middle of the plants has been converted to the showplace of Pierre Bergé and the late Yves Saint-Laurent's art collection. Now called the Museum of Islamic Arts, the assembly features distinctive Moroccan pieces from all over the country. ⓐ Majorelle Gardens, av. Yacoub el Mansour ① 05 24 30 18 52 ① 08.00–12.00, 14.00–18.30

⬆ *The distinctive home of the Museum of Islamic Arts*

RETAIL THERAPY

Atika This boutique is always filled with throngs of shoppers who come to purchase leather designer-inspired shoes in a wide variety of styles and colours. ⓐ 34 rue de la Liberté ⓣ 05 24 43 64 09 ⓑ 09.00–12.30, 15.00–19.30 Mon–Sat

Centre Commercial Just off the main boulevard is the Centre Commercial. Located within an office block and mostly full of souvenirs, this collection of shops is nowhere near as comprehensive as the souks of the Medina. Nevertheless, if time is pressing, and opportunity doesn't allow for meandering, most tourist goods can be purchased here. ⓐ rue Ibn Toumert ⓑ Most stores: 09.00–19.00

Intensité Nomade One of the more expensive boutiques selling Moroccan-influenced fashion made from the finest natural materials. Clothing for both men and women in stock. ⓐ 139 av. Mohammed V ⓣ 05 24 43 13 33 ⓑ 09.00–12.30, 15.00–19.30 Mon–Sat

Librairie ACR Find the art publication you've been looking for at this specialist bookshop. Pick up a book on cooking or design while you're here, and maybe even a postcard or two. ⓐ blvd Mohammed Zerktouni, residence Tayeb ⓣ 05 24 44 67 92 ⓑ 09.00–12.30, 15.00–19.00 Mon–Sat

Maison Rouge Two floors of modern Moroccan designs for the home, including linens, furniture, baskets, tablewares and candles. This French-owned shop appeals to those who like more streamlined designs. ⓐ 6 rue de la Liberté ⓣ 05 24 44 81 30 ⓑ 09.00–13.30, 15.30–19.30 Mon–Sat

SIDI GHANEM

About 20 minutes out of the city centre on the boulevard de Safi by car is Sidi Ghanem or Marrakech's Industrial Zone. Nestled in between the smoke stacks are a number of showrooms with wares for export or destined for the city's upscale restaurants and *riads*. Serious shoppers should set aside a morning or afternoon for browsing, and check out the following:

Akkal Modern Moroccan pottery streamlined to fit the tastes of those who believe less is more. A wide range of colours and shapes is on offer. ⓐ 322 QI Sidi Ghanem ⓣ 05 24 33 59 38 ⓦ www.akkal.net ⓛ 09.00–18.00 Mon–Sat

Fan Wa Nour Part art gallery, part boutique. Unusual and surprising interiors, owned by a French designer. ⓐ 16 bis QI Sidi Ghanem ⓣ 05 24 33 69 60 ⓛ 09.30–18.00 Mon–Fri, 09.30–13.00 Sat

Maison Méditerranéenne A huge showroom filled to the brim with everything to furnish your home Moroccan-style. ⓐ 230 QI Sidi Ghanem ⓣ 05 24 33 60 00/01 ⓛ 08.30–12.30, 14.00–18.00 Mon–Sat

Nour Bougie Selling nothing but Moroccan-inspired candles in a vast number of sizes and shades. ⓐ 231 QI Sidi Ghanem ⓣ 05 24 33 57 18 ⓦ www.nourbougie.com ⓛ 09.00–18.00 Mon–Sat

Via Notti Exquisite bed linens in a variety of styles. ⓐ 322 QI Sidi Ghanem ⓣ 05 24 35 60 24 ⓛ 09.00–13.00, 14.00–18.00 Mon–Fri, 09.00–13.00 Sat

◀ *The Centre Commercial is a good place to find souvenirs*

Mamounia Arts A branch of the famous hotel's art gallery is located in the heart of Guéliz. Fine collectables are on display, including jewellery, arms and 'old curiosities'. ⓐ 7 rue de la Liberté ⓣ 05 24 42 02 00 ⓛ 08.00–20.00

Michéle Bacconier Unusual Moroccan slippers, exotic embroidered *suzanis* (needlework), and other unusual textiles. ⓐ 6 rue du Vieux Marrakchi, off rue de la Liberté ⓣ 05 24 44 91 78 ⓛ 09.00–19.30 Mon–Sat, 09.00–12.30 Sun

L'Orientaliste A charming mixed bag of a place, with old bottles, copper bowls, candlesticks, early 20th-century engravings, Fez pottery, furniture, perfume and all sorts of antiques. There are two locations on the same street. ⓐ 11 & 15 rue de la Liberté ⓣ 05 24 43 40 74 ⓛ 09.00–12.30, 15.00–19.30 Mon–Sat, 09.00–13.00 Sun

Place Vendome Beautiful leather and fine fashion items are for sale in this well-known shop. Though not as cheap as in the souks, the quality is better. ⓐ 141 av. Mohammed V ⓣ 05 24 43 52 63 ⓛ 09.00–12.30, 15.00–19.30 Mon–Sat, 09.00–13.00 Sun

Scènes de Lin An interior decorator's paradise, Anne-Marie Chaoui shows her beautiful products, including fabrics and furniture, to a discerning, and wealthy, clientele. ⓐ 70 rue de la Liberté ⓣ 05 24 43 61 08 ⓛ 09.00–12.30, 15.00–19.30 Mon–Sat

TAKING A BREAK

Amandine £ ❶ Grab a mouth-watering pastry to take away from the well-stocked patisserie, or sit down and enjoy a coffee or snack at the space next door. ② 177 rue Mohammed el-Beqal ❶ 05 24 44 96 12 🕐 07.00–21.30

Boule de Neige £ ❷ The usual range of patisserie-goodies and drinks, both cold and hot, is available, but the biggest draw is the air conditioning, particularly in the summer. ② 30 rue de Yougoslavie ❶ 05 24 44 60 44 🕐 07.00–23.00

Café du Livre £ ❸ A fantastic spot in the city, this café offers a wide range of English-language books to peruse while enjoying coffee, lunch, or an early dinner. Alcoholic drinks are also served here and guests can enjoy Wi-Fi in the comfortable chairs in the café's back area. ② 44 rue Tarik Ben Ziyad ❶ 05 24 43 21 49 🕐 09.00–21.00 Mon–Sat

Glacier Oliveri £ ❹ The ice cream is famous, but the pastries here are also delicious. Come for breakfast, too. ② 7–9 blvd el Mansour Eddahbi ❶ 05 24 44 89 13 🕐 06.00–23.00

Kechmara £ ❺ With a changing art exhibit, this restaurant is the perfect choice for lunch when shopping in the new city. The stylish mid-century modern décor sets it apart from the usual Moroccan choices and the terrace on the roof serves a particularly good mixed grill. ② 3 rue de la Liberté ❶ 05 24 42 25 32 🕐 07.00–00.00 Mon–Sat, 09.00–19.30 Sun

Venezia Ice £ ❻ Perfect for a last-minute treat before catching the train. The flavours are creative and delicious, and the scoops very reasonably priced. ② Railway station, corner av. Hassan II & Mohammed VI ❶ 05 24 45 83 45 🕐 07.00–00.00

La Table du Marché ££ ❼ In the Hivernage area, this charming canopied outdoor restaurant is a delightful spot for lunch. Good salads and pasta dishes. ⓐ Hôtel Hivernage, 4 rue des Temples ❶ 05 24 42 41 00 12 ⓛ 11.00–00.00

AFTER DARK

RESTAURANTS

16eme £ ❽ Visit this modern restaurant for international cuisine and contemporary design. ⓐ Marrakech Plaza, opposite post office ❶ 05 24 33 96 70 ⓛ 07.00–22.00

Café de la Poste £ ❾ More a restaurant than a café, this place has excellent hot lunch and dinner options as well as salads and sandwiches. In the spring or summer, enjoy a beer on the covered terrace. ⓐ Corner blvd Mansour Eddahbi & av. Imam Malik, pl. du 16 Novembre, Gueliz ❶ 05 24 43 30 38 ⓛ 08.00–00.00

Rotisserie de la Paix £ ❿ As the name says, the speciality of this outdoor venue is various types of meat grilled over a wood fire. In the shade at lunchtime, or under the lights in the evening, sitting in the garden is always pleasant. ⓐ 68 rue de Yougoslavie ❶ 05 24 43 31 18 ⓛ 12.00–15.00, 19.00–23.00

Bo & Zin ££ ⓫ Just a little way out of the city, this very stylish restaurant serves passable Thai and fusion fare. A seat in the garden is a particularly lovely setting for drinks with friends. ⓐ route de l'Ourika ❶ 05 24 38 80 13 ⓛ 21.00–01.00

Crystal Restaurant Lounge ££ **12** On the outskirts of the city and in the trendy Pacha complex, this restaurant offers fine dining in a lovely art deco setting. Make a reservation for Friday or Saturday night to listen to solo jazz artists live. ⓐ Pacha, av. Mohammed VI, l'Aguedal ⓣ 05 24 38 84 00 ⓛ 21.00–00.00

Lolo Quoi ££ **13** This fashionable restaurant has a club-like feeling to it and is one of the spots where the Marrakchi beautiful people gather. The food is good but the music can be quite loud after 22.00. ⓐ av. Hassan II ⓣ 072 56 98 64 ⓛ 21.00–00.00

La Trattoria ££ **14** Some of the best Italian dishes in the city are complemented by the Hispano-Moorish 1920s-style decor. Outdoor tables flank the pool, while the rooms in which the indoor ones sit are legendary. ⓐ 179 rue Mohammed el-Beqal ⓣ 05 24 43 26 41 ⓦ www.latrattoriamarrakech.com ⓛ 19.00–23.30

La Villa ££ **15** With an excellent French chef, this restaurant in the Hivernage area is a pleasure for the eyes and the palate. Romantic seating outdoors in a private setting. ⓐ av. du President Kennedy, across from Hotel Kenza Fara ⓣ 05 24 42 19 69 ⓛ 20.00–00.00

BARS, CLUBS & DISCOS
Le Diamont Noir With a less expensive entrance charge than the fashionable clubs, this hang-out attracts a varied crowd, more interested in having a good time than with looks. There's also an active gay scene here. ⓐ Hotel Le Marrakech, pl. de la Liberté ⓣ 05 24 43 43 51 ⓛ 22.00–dawn

Jad Mahal People of all ages will feel comfortable coming to this venue in the Hivernage area. The décor is heavy on the Moroccan fantasy theme, complete with belly dancers who make their appearance late in the evening. ⓐ 10 rue Haroun Errachid ⓣ 05 24 43 69 84 ⓛ 20.00–02.00

Montecristo Salsa and samba dominate the upstairs dance floor, while the rooftop is the place to sip cocktails or down a beer. Nibble on some tapas, or take a puff on a cigar, both for sale here. ⓐ 20 rue Ibn Äicha ⓣ 05 24 43 90 31 ⓛ 19.00–02.00

Pacha One of the newest, biggest, and hippest clubs in town, Pacha is part of the famous chain with venues in Ibiza, London and New York. The club often has feature performers and the house DJ spins a mix of local and international favourites. ⓐ av. Mohammed VI, l'Aguedal ⓣ 06 61 10 28 87 ⓛ 00.00–dawn

Le Theatro Just next to the Hotel Saadi's casino, the club's DJ plays an eclectic range of music, ranging from techno and house to Moroccan and R'n'B. ⓐ av. el Quadissia, Hivernage ⓣ 06 64 86 03 39

CINEMAS

Cinéma Rif This 800-seat movie house plays the usual range of films suited to the Moroccan taste, taken from both Asian and Western traditions. ⓐ Cité Mohammadia (near the Palmeraie) ⓣ 05 24 30 31 46

La Colisée A comfortable and popular venue for cinema. ⓐ blvd Mohammed Zerktouni ⓣ 05 24 44 88 93

PALMERAIE

Luxury: some of us are born to it, most of us dream of it. What is certain is that we all deserve it, and, at the rich desert resort of Palmeraie, visitors can really experience it. This legendary palm grove (hence the name) is a glittering oasis of desert opulence, some 20 km (12 miles) to the northeast of Marrakech, on the route de Casablanca. Home to the best-heeled elements of the native and expat population, the area sparkles with luxury hotels, nightlife and spas. All you need to partake of its pleasures (if only voyeuristically) is the chutzpah to leap onto one of the camels that lurk lugubriously around the resort's periphery and the confidence to let it transport you to the world within.

Once you've trotted through the back nine on the golf course at the Palmeraie Golf Palace (see page 40), you could work off the nibbles you sampled in each of the resort's eight restaurants with a boogie in one of its exclusive nightclubs (providing you'd been able to find something to wear in one of the boutiques in its shopping centre). Then again, if you were a little self-indulgent in the 2-Michelin-star **Dar Ennassim** restaurant (☎ 05 24 33 43 08 ⏱ 07.30–10.30, 12.30–14.30, 19.30–late ❶ Reservations recommended), perhaps a gentle width of one of the oceanic pools in Le Nikki Beach (see page 43) will put you back in the pink. Heady with post-exercise euphoria, why not book a tent (yes, a tent, but it's not like any you saw in the Girl Guides) at the Palais Rhoul (see page 41)? They take pets there, so you can let the camel loose on its perfectly-manicured lawns. After all, you don't want him getting the hump.

Mégarama Theatre With nine screens, you're sure to find something of interest. ➋ Off the Jardins de l'Aguedal ☏ 08 90 10 20 20 🌐 www.megarama.info

EVENTS & SHOWS

Al Ménara Using the latest sound and light technology, this show combines visual effects with live performers to produce a magnificent outdoor show at the Ménara Gardens. Reflections in the large pool double the effect. ➋ Ménara Gardens 🕐 21.00 Wed–Mon, Mar–Dec

Chez Ali Ostensibly a tourist version of the Festival of Popular Arts, the dinner combo takes elements from Moroccan culture and the *One Thousand and One Nights* tales and puts on a show of dance, music and folklore. The horsemanship is pretty amazing. ➋ Circuit de la Palmeraie ☏ 05 24 30 77 30 🌐 www.ilove-marrakesh.com/chezali

▶ *Sunset is the time for a camel ride on the beach at Essaouira*

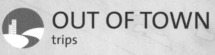

OUT OF TOWN
trips

The High Atlas Mountains

Even on summer days it's impossible not to be aware of the mountainous backdrop to the city of Marrakech, and on winter ones the snow-covered High Atlas Mountains are extremely impressive. The alpine-like environment is as close as it looks, as it's less than 100 km (about 60 miles) from the city to the base of Mount Toubkal, North Africa's tallest mountain at 4,167 m (13,670 ft). In fact, within minutes of driving south of Marrakech the landscape changes to that of rural Morocco. Soon, the contours begin appearing, along with terraced fields and villages that seem to be carved out of the hills themselves. The roads get narrower and the scenery and views become increasingly dramatic as the road passes through small market towns. Within a couple of hours, the landscape becomes rugged and truly mountainous, equally spectacular in the warm haze of summer or the chilly frost of winter.

GETTING THERE

Four main routes lead to the Atlas, two of which continue to destinations on the other side of the range, and two that go no further. The most easterly is the Tizi n'Tichka road, a dramatic and fairly safe highway that leads to the city of Ouarzazate, 225 km (140 miles) away, and points further south. The furthest west is the drive that goes as far south as Amizmiz, about 55 km (34 miles) from Marrakech, passing the village of Tamesloht and its interesting Kasbah, as well as the Lalla Takerkoust Dam and reservoir.

The middle two thoroughfares are the ones that are the most worthwhile for short trips. The Tizi n' Test is a difficult but interesting road that leads to Taroudant, three and a half hours away, but before

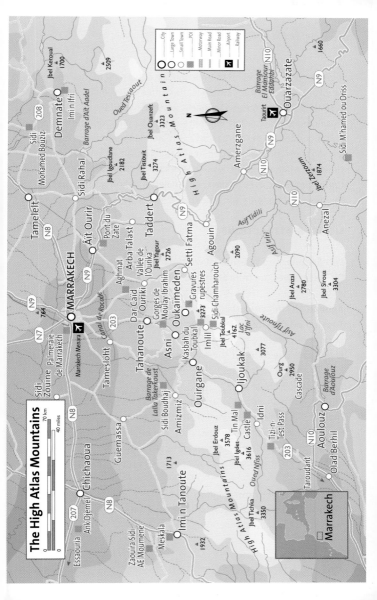

it gets tricky, branches off to Imlil and the beginning of the Mount Toubkal ascent. Another option is the Ourika Valley and town of Setti Fatma, about 62 km (39 miles) away, although the ski resort of Oukaïmeden is accessible beforehand via a turn-off along this road.

It's possible to get to most of the major destinations via bus, leaving from the main station near Bab Doukkala in Marrakech. However, when travelling by public transport, you are subject to local timetables that can be inconvenient. A better option is to hire a grand taxi, negotiating fares and rendezvous points with the drivers.

SIGHTS & ATTRACTIONS

Listed below are a selection of worthwhile towns in the area. Distances given are from Marrakech.

Aghmat (21 km/13 miles)
Turn left off the Ourika Valley Road to reach the remains of an ancient Almoravid city. The grave of the 11th-century poet king El Moutamid rests in the town, together with his shrine.

Asni (45 km/28 miles)
The largest town along the Tizi n' Test Road is famous for its Saturday market. Full of local produce, livestock and Moroccan 'food halls', the bazaar provides a fascinating insight into rural life. Look out for the donkey, aka Berber Mercedes, 'parking lot'. Asni itself is pleasant enough and offers great views of the towering peaks surrounding the place.

Dar Caïd Ouriki (40 km/25 miles)
This town comes into its own on Mondays, when it stages a weekly market for the inhabitants of this area.

SKIING IN AFRICA

One of the most exotic, not to mention unusual, places in the world for winter sports is at Oukaïmeden, just outside Marrakech. Situated on a mountain whose peak is at an altitude of 3,258 m (10,689 ft), and with a vertical drop of 663 m (2,175 ft) and 20 pistes measuring 20 km (12 miles) in total, this French-developed resort can be a fine place to ski when the snowfall is decent (the pistes are not very challenging). There is also sledding and sled rental.

Donkeys supply a uniquely Moroccan touch, providing transport to runs that the lifts don't service. Passes and ski equipment rental are very reasonably priced but not terribly good quality. When there is snow, the resort can get pretty crowded on weekends, when the Marrakchis take advantage of their proximity and get in all the skiing they can.

Imlil (62 km/39 miles)

Turning left at the fork from Asni, and following it to the end of the paved road, you come to this thriving little town in the heart of the High Atlas foothills. Serving as a centre for all the Berber villages that lie along the crests and high up in the mountains, Imlil is a microcosm of a big town, with most goods and facilities that locals might want, albeit on a miniature scale. Even primary schools are provided (the closest secondary is in Asni). Imlil and the nearby Kasbah du Toubkal are excellent bases for hikes into the peaks, including the ascent of Mount Toubkal. Guides and provisions can be acquired here.

Kasbah du Toubkal (70 km/43 miles)
The owners have renovated this hilltop citadel and done a magnificent job. Framed against the background of North Africa's highest peaks, the massive construction serves as a hotel, restaurant, hammam and hiking centre. Single and multi-day trips with Berber guides can be organised (see page 123 for more information).

Moulay Ibrahim (38 km/24 miles)
Just past Tahanoute on a side road is a little enclave famous for its eponymous shrine, and the pilgrims who come from all around to see it. A *moussem*, or organised pilgrimage, takes place every year. Of more interest to non-Muslims are the gorges that are just to the north of the hamlet.

Ouirgane (60 km/37 miles)
This little village among the pine trees, on the main Tizi n' Test road, is known as an excellent starting point for Atlas treks, as well as for delightful guesthouses. It's a good place from which to hike or horseback ride, where it's still possible to spend the night in comfort.

Oukaïmeden (77 km/48 miles)
Morocco's main ski resort lies at the heart of the High Atlas Range, at an altitude of 2,600 m (8,530 ft). Between December and March enough snow usually falls to cover the entire region and allow the chairlifts, rope tows and equipment rental to operate. Accommodation is available in various styles, ranging from a 4-star luxury hotel

---

● *Oukaïmeden is the country's main ski resort*

to a mountain refuge. In the summer, the area is much less visited, although quite a few hikes begin from here.

Setti Fatma (62 km/39 miles)

At the end of the Ourika Valley, as well as the road, is this village known for its saint and the *moussem* (pilgrimage) held in his honour every year in August. More of a fair than a religious event, it attracts families as well as the occasional mystic. For the rest of the year, the place is better known for its seven *cascades* (waterfalls). To visit, hire one of the readily available local guides.

⬇ *The market comes to the mountains at Tahanoute*

MARKET DAYS

Much of the region's buying activity is done through the weekly markets. Although not really for tourists, the bazaars are extremely interesting, especially for experiencing a bit of local life. The days for some of the larger town's gatherings are:

Aghmat Friday
Asni Saturday
Dar Caid Ourika Monday
Ouirgane Thursday
Setti Fatma Thursday
Tahanoute Tuesday & Saturday

Tahanoute (32 km/20 miles)

Lying at 1,000 m (3,300 ft) above sea level, with the Reghaia river below, this little village comes to life on Tuesdays and Saturdays, when it stages its enormous rural market.

Tin Mal (100 km/62 miles)

The 12th-century Almohad dynasty began life here, revering this little town as its holy city. Sections of the original medieval ramparts are still visible. They are, however, overshadowed by the restored mosque that non-Muslims are allowed to visit.

RETAIL THERAPY

Alongside the roads are several small shops selling ammonites, trilobites and 'minerals' that come from the deserts of south Morocco. The fossils are usually real, although a certain amount of perusing

can determine if they're fake. The 'minerals' are very often rocks that have been artificially coloured or enhanced. Be very wary regarding their authenticity, and unless you are sure they're genuine or simply like the look of them, don't buy them.

Carpet sellers peddle their wares all over Morocco, and the road to the Atlas is one of their strongholds. The floor mats are usually legitimate, and often quite beautiful, but the sales patter can be a bit overwhelming. However, if you're sincerely interested in purchasing rugs, the mountains can be a good location to acquire them. It's best to do some research in Marrakech to discover the going rate, before practising bargaining in the highlands.

TAKING A BREAK

Café Soleil £ This café is where visitors and locals hang out in Imlil, usually on the outdoor terrace. Reasonably priced rooms are another of the services offered. ❸ Centre of Imlil ❶ 05 24 48 56 22 ❶ 07.30–19.00

Au Sanglier Qui Fume £ This basic lodge is located on the Tizi n'Test road, about 60 km (37 miles) south of Marrakech. With pleasant surroundings and a covered terrace, it's a nice place to stop for lunch. Accommodation and dinner are also available. ❸ On the left in the village of Ouirgane ❶ 05 24 48 57 07 ❿ www.ausanglierquifume.com ❶ 12.00–15.00, 19.30–22.00

Tichka Atlas £ With views of the valley below, and the Berber villages above, this restaurant is well located for a break between the morning and afternoon hikes. ❸ 400 m (437 yds) from the centre of Imlil, route de Tachedirte ❶ 05 24 48 52 23 ❶ 07.00–22.00

ACCOMMODATION

Auberge le Maquis £ Clean, colourful and with lovely views, this former hunting lodge is a nice base for hiking in the Ourika Valley. The price includes dinner or lunch. ❸ Aghbalou, vallée de l'Ourika, km 45 ❶ 05 24 48 45 31 ❾ www.le-maquis.com

Chez Momo £ Experience a real Berber ambience in this charming little rural inn, nestling at the base of the Atlas and serving authentic regional cuisine. Momo was born in the village and reveres the tradition of hospitality. ❸ Ourigane ❶ 05 24 48 57 04 ❾ www.aubergemomo.com

Club Alpin Français £ This organisation runs several refuges in the area, in association with the Youth Hostel Association. Used mostly for overnight stays for trekkers, the accommodation consists primarily of multi-bedded dorm rooms. ❶ 023 45 93 97 ❾ www.caf-maroc.com

Hotel Etoile du Toubkal £ Cheap and cheerful, this basic hotel is located right in the heart of the village. A few rooms have baths. ❸ Imlil ❶ 05 24 48 56 18

Chez Juju ££ A reasonable place to stay for a ski break: the price of an overnight stay at this very good hotel, in the centre of Oukaïmeden, includes full board. Skis, poles and boots are available for hire in the nearby shops. ❸ Station de Ski, Oukaïmeden ❶ 05 24 31 90 05

Kasbah du Toubkal ££ This beautifully renovated Kasbah sits on a hill (hike or mule ride required) at the base of Mount Toubkal. Room options range from shared dorms to entire apartments. The Kasbah

⬆ *Kasbah du Toubkal offers elegant accommodation, and meals*

also offers lunch and dinner, and guided tours to the neighbouring villages, as well as treks into the mountains. Winner of a Green Globe Award for Sustainable Tourism. ⓐ Imlil ⓣ 05 24 43 85 04 ⓦ www.kasbahdutoubkal.com

Kenzi Louka ££ At an altitude of 2,600 m (8,530 ft), this 4-star hotel in the Oukaïmeden ski area looks just like an upmarket French resort, with all its facilities. It's open all year, although its high season is the winter. ⓐ Oukaïmeden ⓣ 05 24 31 90 80 ⓦ www.kenzi-hotels.com

Kasbah Tamadot £££ Owned by Sir Richard Branson, this Kasbah, 45 minutes from Marrakech, offers luxurious rooms, a pool with mountain views as well as an indoor pool, tennis courts, and a spa. Hot-air ballooning (not surprisingly), horseback riding and trekking can be organised. ⓐ Asni ⓣ 05 24 36 82 00 ⓦ www.kasbahtamadot.virgin.com

Residence La Roseraie £££ This fabulous residence is an exercise in luxury. With a spa, three pools, private terraces, excellent food and horse riding, staying here is truly an indulgence. Save up your dirhams and spend a few delicious days here. ⓐ Ourigane ⓣ 05 24 43 91 28 ⓛ Restaurant: 12.00–15.00, 19.30–22.00

Essaouira

Charming, cooled by constant ocean breezes, and with a relaxed atmosphere, this seaside town, 170 km (105 miles) from Marrakech, still has enough going on to make it a happening place. Much smaller and certainly lower-key than Marrakech, Essaouira's distinctive colours and lovely location attract both foreign and domestic artists and tourists. Buildings painted blue and white are complemented by the occasional splash of yellow. Craftsmen sell their wares in the Medina and underneath the town walls, while painters exhibit their work both in galleries and the Medina's streets. Located on a rocky outcrop extending into the Atlantic Ocean, one of the town's outstanding features is its 18th-century rampart that not only protects the city's heart but also functions as a maritime battlement. Fortified to prevent successful attacks from the sea, the row of cannons that peaks out through gaps in the barriers is one of the more interesting legacies.

Essaouira's location has made it a viable port since Phoenician times. Visited by representatives from most of the ancient Mediterranean powers, Romans set up a trading post during the first century BC. A factory was established when the inhabitants discovered that the local purpura shells could be ground up and made into a royal purple colour. Called Amogdoul after an 11th-century saint, Sidi Mogdoul, who was buried there, the early 16th-century Portuguese invaders renamed it Mogador. By the mid-century, the Moroccans claimed back the city, and 200 years later, in 1776, the sultan used the skills of a French engineer, captured during a failed invasion, to redesign the city. For a while the town was known as Saouira, 'the small fortress', but gradually changed to 'Es-Saouira', 'the beautifully designed', after its transformation. In its heyday, the port was the

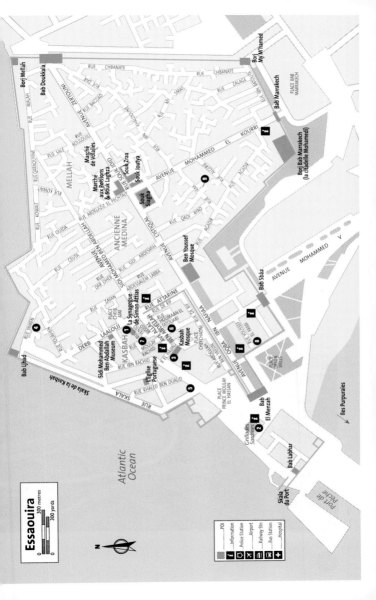

Essaouira

0 ——— 300 metres
0 ——— 300 yards

N

Atlantic Ocean

RUE CHBANATE

RUE CHBANATE

RUE ZAR

RUE ZALACE

Borj Mellah

Bab Doukkala

RUE MALAH

RUE BACHAD

AVENUE ZERTOUNI

RUE BOULOUJE

MELLAH

RUE CARBOUYINE

RUE SALE

RUE KOUWAIT

RUE OUJDA

RUE CEUTA

RUE KAWAIT

Marché de Volailles

Marché aux Poissons & Souk Laghza

Souk Jdid

Souk Zraa

Souk Joutya

Souk Siagha

ANCIENNE MEDINA

AVENUE BEN ABDELLAH

RUE ABDELAZIZ EL FECHTALY

RUE DAR DHEBBAGH

RUE SIDI ABDESMIH

AVENUE L'ISTIQLAL

AVENUE MOHAMMED EL KOURRI

RUE AGADIR

RUE QADI AYAD

RUE AGADIR

RUE AGADIR

AVENUE MOHAMMED V

Ben Youssef Mosque

Bab Skâa

9

Borj My M'hamed

Bab Marrakech

PLACE BAB MARRAKECH

Borj Bab Marrakech (la citadelle Mohamedi)

PLACE MARRAKECH

2 i

RUE ZAVAN

RUE KABEN

Bab Ljhad

4

DERB

PLACE CHRIB ATAI

1 La Synagogue de Simon Attias

i

RUE ATTARINE

RUE DE RIF

RUE LAALOUJ

RUE MOULAY RACHID

Sidi Mohammed Ben Abdallah Museum

7

6

RUE HOURRANE EL FAIHATE

Kasbah Mosque

3

i

PLACE CHRIB ATAI

RUE CHECHAONI

RUE DE LA SKALA

RUE IBN ROCHD

Eglise Portugaise

RUE KHALED BEN OUALID

5

PLACE PRINCE MOULAY EL HASSAN

AVENUE DE L'ISTIQLAL

RUE OQBA

RUE IBN KHALDOUN

RUE DE LA SKALA

SKALA

Skala de la kasbah

RUE RABEN

Bab Sbâa

AVENUE MOHAMMED V

i 2

i

8

PLACE ORSON WELLS

Iles Purpurales

i 2 Bab El Menzah

Grillades Souiries

Bab Labhar

Skala du Port

Port de pêche

i Information
Police Station
Airport
Railway Stn
Bus Station
+ Hospital
POI

main outlet for the Timbuktu caravans. The development of the larger Agadir drew trade away from Essaouira and slowly the smaller town was reduced to being merely a fishing port. Tourism, however, began and has now evolved into a major economic force.

In the 1950s, the director and actor Orson Welles succumbed to Essaouira's appeal and used its walls in his film *Othello*. In the 1960s, the city was discovered as part of the Hippy Trail, and its most famous visitor from this era was Jimi Hendrix (as placards in various places within the Medina will not let 21st-century tourists forget!). Although still retaining its charm, development is continuing, mostly outside the Medina. The ocean provides some of the best windsurfing in North Africa, and hotels and resorts are being constructed to cater to this new source of revenue. For those less willing to brave the cold Atlantic waters,

beachside horse and camel riding are available a brief stroll away from the city centre.

GETTING THERE

From place du 16 Novembre in the heart of Marrakech's new city, follow avenue Hassan II west past the train station. Thereafter Hassan II becomes route P10, and you should continue for 197 km (122 miles) through the towns of Oudaya, Chichaoua and Ounagha. When you have run out of road and hit the chilly Atlantic, you are there. Once you've passed Oudaya, do watch out for goats (of the tree-climbing variety), who stand in the road munching leaves.

◆ *This seaside resort is also a working fishing port*

SIGHTS & ATTRACTIONS

Babs

The Medina, or ancient centre, is protected by a complete wall with various entry points, or *babs*, providing access to the heart. Some of these openings are very dramatic, including:

Bab Doukkala Lying at the city's northeastern edge, this gate dates back to Essaouira's 18th-century facelift and was designed to be its principal entrance.

Bab Labhar Also known as the Porte de la Marine, this impressive arch is the gateway to the fishing harbour from the Medina.

Bab Marrakech The only breach in the wall built for defence against attacks from the east, various artists and artisans now reside and display in this area.

Bab Sbâa Leading directly to avenue Mohammed V, the main highway from both Marrakech and Agadir, this portal is the one that most visitors see first.

Beach

The beautiful west-facing strand extends for miles. Protected by islands in the bay, the sea is normally relatively flat and it's a pleasure to wade through the gentle surf. Together with the constant breezes, the town has developed an excellent reputation for windsurfing, with facilities and rentals widely available. Some beachside hotels cater especially for the sport. Further along the bay, horses and camels wait for tourists to enjoy the stroll on four legs (try Argaibi Mohammed ☎ 070 57 79 41).

Ben Youssef Mosque

Laid out in traditional fashion and located on the Medina's main

ESSAOUIRA'S WIND SPORTS

Thanks to its geographical location, Essaouira has winds almost all year round, which is why it's known as 'the windy city'. Thus it's become a hub for kite surfing and sail boarding, surfing and car-kite sailing. The city hosted the Kiteboard World Cup in 2007 and has been an increasingly important stop on the Kiteboard Pro World Tour since 1999. There are numerous surf shops near the beach where you can rent equipment and take lessons, so why not slip into a wetsuit, hope for a fair wind and prepare for lift-off?

boulevard is one of the most important and impressive mosques in the city (not open to non-Muslims). ❷ av. l'Istiqlal

L'Eglise Portuguese
West of the Medina lies the remains of this richly decorated Catholic church, established by the first European businessmen who settled here in the 18th century. It is no longer a functioning church. ❷ Near Skala de la Kasbah, off rue Khaled Ben Oualid

Iles Purpuraies
A series of little islands out to the west of the bay provides not only cover for the beach, but also a lovely backdrop, especially as the sun goes down. Now designated as an area of special scientific interest, landing visits are not allowed, although it is possible to sail in the area. Vestiges of ancient habitation remain, including ruins of the purpure (purple) factories, and a Portuguese fort on the Island of Mogador.

Kasbah Mosque

Just off the main square, the mosque dates back to the days of the city's reconstruction (not open to non-Muslims). ⓐ off pl. Prince Moulay el Hassan

Place Prince Moulay El Hassan

At the southern end of the Medina is a main square that leads down to the port. The largest open space within the old city, here is where many outdoor cafés and restaurants reside. Always buzzing, this spot is ideal for breakfast, mid-morning coffee, light lunch, afternoon mint tea, or even a bit of sunset watching.

Port de Pêche

Dramatically guarded by the centuries-old Porte de la Marine, the fishing port is a fascinating place. When the boats come in, the activity is raucous, fishermen unloading their often exotic catch, seagulls squawking in hope and both tourists and locals standing around to watch. At other times, nets are strewn about with men rapidly unwinding or repairing them. Most interesting, however, is the traditional boat-building and repair. Up on plinths, vessels in various sizes and colours, and in all states of assembly and renovation, dominate the skyline of the harbour.

Religious buildings

Some of the different faiths practised in Essaouira in the past are still represented by their prayer houses. The city today has 18 mosques, 15 *zaouias* (tombs of saints, including Sidi Magdoul, the one who gave the city its previous names), two Catholic churches and four synagogues.

⬤ *Fortifications – skalas – protected Essaouira from invasion in the 18th century*

Skalas

These coastal fortifications are probably the most distinctive feature of Essaouira. Part of the 18th-century redesign of the city, the barrier walls were constructed as defenses, acting as protection against invasions from the sea, and additionally enforced with cannons pointing out towards their attackers. At various points are *borjs*, fortifications that further enforce security.

Skala de la Kasbah

The southwest-facing barrier offers not only a sense of safety to the inhabitants within its shadow, but also a delightful wall-top path overlooking the sea. Along the edges are pieces of installed weaponry, while underneath, in the arches, are the studios and shops of wood workers and cabinet makers.

Skala du Port

Towering over the fishing port, this huge and intriguing fortification offers great views of both the activities below and the ocean beyond. For a small fee, it's possible to see the construction from the inside.
🕐 08.00–12.00, 14.00–18.00

Souks

Much more easygoing than Marrakech, walking through Essaouira's souks is a pleasure. Meandering and maze-like, the shopping experience provides a sense of exploration and discovery. Although based mostly along the main street, shops and markets sprawl all over the town. Some of the specialist areas are: Fabric market (Souk Joutya); Fish market (Marché aux Poissons); Grain market (Souk Zraa); Jewellery market (Souk Siagha); and the Spice market (Souk Laghza).

La Synagogue de Simon Attias

Essaouira was a trading city and many of its inhabitants were Jews, living primarily in the Mellah, at the north end of the Medina. Most left by the 1960s, migrating to other countries, especially Israel or the United States. This 19th-century remainder in the heart of the Medina is one of the few synagogues that still stands. ⓐ rue Yetno Besed, Kasbah

CULTURE

Art galleries

The city is famous for its artists and there are several formal art galleries, as well as impromptu displays laid out on the streets. Some of the venues double as shops, while others are purely exhibition areas. The Taros Café (see page 138) presents world music and musical evenings alongside its visual arts and commercial interests.

The **Exposition de l'Ensemble Artisanal** (ⓐ av. Mohammed el Kourri, Bab Marrakech) is another place to see traditional, handmade crafts and get a guide to the quality and price of items out in the souks.

Gnaoua festival

This festival, held annually in June, celebrates Gnaoua, a traditional music genre that has captured the imagination of many of the West's more mainstream musicians. For four days, exponents of the pure form show off their technique while foreign performers join in to create fusion. Started in 1998, this event has been gaining momentum, becoming more popular, and more crowded, every year. ⓦ www.festival-gnaoua.co.ma

Sidi Mohammed Ben Abdallah Museum (Musée des Arts et Traditions Populaires)

Named after the sultan who commissioned the 18th-century redesign of the city, this museum is the only formal one in town. It specialises in Moroccan ethnography and includes displays on musical instruments, 19th- and 20th-century fashion, mostly silver jewellery and furniture constructed from the local *thuya* wood. ⓐ 7 Derb Laalouj ⓣ 05 24 47 53 00 ⓛ 08.30–18.30 Thur–Tues

RETAIL THERAPY

Arga'Dor Various products made with the oil from the fruit of the native Argan tree are for sale here, including soaps, scents and even honey. ⓐ 5 rue Ibn Rachid, Medina ⓣ 06 61 60 14 71

L'Art du Bain Artisan soap makers create bars in all shapes and sizes and in a huge range of fabulous scents – go in for a sniff. ⓐ 41 rue Skala ⓣ 06 68 44 59 42 (also in Marrakech ⓐ 32 Marché Central de Guéliz, rue Ibn Toummert ⓣ 06 68 44 59 42)

● *Essaouira offers a wide range of water and wind sports*

Bazar Tilili Pottery items are stacked up and crammed into every available space, in both the traditional Fes, and the more modern Safi styles. ⓐ 55 rue Souk Jdid ⓣ 06 68 94 50 66

Chez Samir All sorts of Moroccan bits and pieces are sold, ranging from carpets to artisan objects. Most interesting are the coloured powders from which artists' paints are made, including the ground-up shell Murex blue. ⓐ 16 rue Ibn Rachid, Medina ⓣ 06 68 51 77 67

Galerie Bouafia Beautiful paintings and drawings, as well as a smattering of antiques. The artist, after whom the gallery is named, is often in residence with paintbrush in hand. ⓐ 40 rue Skala ⓣ 06 61 70 98 60

TAKING A BREAK

Crêperie Mogador £ ❶ This French-owned place serves delicious lunch and dessert crêpes. Stop by for a snack while shopping. ⓐ 4 Derb Laalouj ⓣ 05 24 88 30 96 ⓛ 12.00–15.00, 19.00–22.00 Sat–Thur

Fish market stalls £ ❷ Between place Moulay Hassan and the port are these stalls where each vendor displays his catch and offers to cook whatever you choose in any quantity in any fashion. Sit at the tables provided and enjoy the freshest fish and seafood imaginable, while watching others do the same. ⓛ 12.00–22.00

Joli Coin £ ❸ Very good pizza and excellent *shwarmas* (meat sandwiches) available to take away. This little place is perfect for

those who want to eat on the cheap. ⓐ rue el Hajjali, pl. Prince Moulay el Hassan ⓣ 05 24 47 37 94 ⓞ 11.00–23.00

Restaurant Il Mare £ ❹ With one of the most beautiful views in the city, and decent pizza, it's worth stopping by this restaurant for a midday break. Have a seat on the uppermost floor. ⓐ 43 rue Yamen ⓣ 05 24 47 6417 ⓞ 12.00–00.00

Taros Café £ ❺ As well as an artistic and musical venue, the café serves alcohol at its bar, together with the more usual beverages – sit below, on the square, or above, on the terrace. ⓐ pl. Prince Moulay el Hassan 2 ⓣ 05 24 47 64 07 ⓦ www.taroscafe.com ⓞ 11.00–16.00, 18.00–00.00

AFTER DARK

La Decouverte £ ❻ This tiny French-owned restaurant boasts inexpensive Moroccan dishes and homemade pasta. Offerings depend on what is fresh in the market. ⓐ 8 bis rue Houmman el Fatouaki ⓣ 05 24 47 31 58 ⓦ www.essaouira-ladecouverte.com ⓞ 12.00–15.00, 19.00–22.00 Sun–Fri

Le Patio £ ❼ Within a *riad*, the tapas restaurant menu changes daily, comprising whatever fish have been taken from the sea that day, as well as the more usual tagines. ⓐ 28 rue Moulay Rachid, Medina ⓣ 05 24 47 41 66 ⓞ 17.00–23.00 Tues–Sun

After Five ££ ❽ With a young French chef, this relaxed but stylish venue offers excellent and creative seafood and other dishes, as well as good wines. The menu changes daily and the chef is happy to make

recommendations. ⓐ 7 rue Youssef el Fassi ⓣ 05 24 47 33 49
ⓛ Restaurant: 12.00–17.00, 19.30–23.00; bar: 12.00–00.00

Passage 24 ££ ⓞ This nicely renovated *riad* is a lovely setting for a
romantic dinner for two. The French couple who own the restaurant
ensure careful service and can provide tips about what to do and
see in town. ⓐ 24 rue Irak ⓣ 05 24 47 33 30 ⓛ 19.00–23.00

ACCOMMODATION

HOTELS

Ibis Moussafir Essaouira £ For a clean, good value basic hotel
you can't go wrong with an Ibis. It is located at the entrance to
Essaouira, about a five-minute drive to the beach. ⓐ route de
Marrakech ⓣ 05 24 47 92 80 ⓦ www.ibishotel.com

Palazzo Desdemona £ (££ suite) Sprawled around a large central
courtyard with each spacious room equipped with a four-poster
bed, this traditionally decorated hotel faces onto the Medina's
main thoroughfare. ⓐ 12–14 rue Youssef el Fassi, Medina
ⓣ 05 24 47 22 27

Riad al Madina £ In a *riad* dating from the late 19th century, though
having gone through various facelifts since then, the hotel is still
famous for some of its 1960s clientele, including Jimi Hendrix,
Jefferson Airplane and Frank Zappa. ⓐ 9 rue Attarine, Medina
ⓣ 05 24 47 59 07 ⓦ www.riadalmadina.com

Madada Mogador ££ Decorated by a famous Moroccan interior
designer, this beautiful small hotel has luxurious rooms and

will not disappoint. The view from the terrace is splendid.
ⓐ 5 rue Youssef el Fassi ⓣ 05 24 47 55 12 ⓦ www.madada.com

Riad Dar Qawi £££ This lovely four-bedroom self-catering
apartment is in the heart of the Medina and has ocean views.
Minimum stay three nights. ⓐ 50 rue Agadir ⓣ +44 7887 700 001
ⓦ www.riadbythesea.com

Sofitel £££ This large 4-star hotel located alongside the sea has full
luxury facilities including a spa and swimming pool, private section
of beach, and windsurfing equipment rental. ⓐ av. Mohammed V
ⓣ 05 24 47 90 00 ⓦ www.accorhotels.com

CAMPSITES

There are several campsites in the general area, although some are
a little way out of town:

Camping le Calme £ A total of 150 spots, including 100 for motor
homes and 50 for tents. ⓐ 15 km (10 miles) southeast from the centre,
on the route to the village of Arba Ida ou Gourd ⓣ 05 24 47 61 96

Camping Tangaro £ Smaller than some of the other sites, there are
80 spaces with 60 for motor homes and 20 for tents. ⓐ 6 km (4 miles)
south on the road to Agadir-Diabat ⓣ 05 24 78 47 84

ⓞ *Surf the net out of doors at Marrakech's Cyber Parc (see page 149)*

PRACTICAL
information

Directory

GETTING THERE

There are various ways to get to Marrakech, depending on how much time you have and how much you would like to see en route.

By air

It's possible to fly nonstop to Marrakech's Menara Airport from London Gatwick, as well as several major European cities, including Paris. Some flights, however, stop over at Casablanca. Airlines that cover this route include **Ryanair** (Ⓦ www.ryanair.com), **easyJet** (Ⓦ www.easyjet.com) and **Royal Air Maroc** (Ⓦ www.royalairmaroc.com). From the USA, Royal Air Maroc has a nonstop routing from JFK Airport in New York to Casablanca, with connections available at either end.

Many people are aware that air travel emits CO_2, which contributes to climate change. You may be interested in the possibility of lessening the environmental impact of your flight through the charity **Climate Care** (Ⓦ www.climatecare.org), which offsets your CO_2 by funding environmental projects around the world.

By rail

All trains that traverse Morocco are domestic. The easiest way to get to Marrakech from Europe is to take the ferry crossing from Spain over the Gibraltar straits to Tangier, and head to Casablanca, from where there is a direct line to the central railway station (see page 59). Although tracks exist, there have been no border crossings from Algeria since 1994. The Moroccan rail network is efficient and has an excellent website at Ⓦ www.oncf.ma

By road

To reach Marrakech by road, take the ferry to Tangier, then the toll motorway from there to Rabat, Casablanca and Marrakech. For more information on driving in Morocco, contact the **Touring Club du Maroc** (🅐 3 av. des FAR, Casablanca ☎ 022 20 30 64).

By water

Several companies make the ferry crossing to Tangier, including **Euroferrys** (🅦 www.euroferrys.com) and **Ferries Rapido del Sur**

🔻 *Blue skies shine through Menara Airport's lattice-effect canopy*

(Ⓦ www.frs.es). Times vary greatly depending on where you travel to and from, and on which type of boat you travel, so do investigate the different options and prices thoroughly before buying your ticket. Catamarans are faster than ordinary ferries but cost a lot more.

Taking the ferry to the quieter port of Ceuta might be a better option when travelling by car, as there is less traffic. However, there are few public transport connections from here to Marrakech. If time is not a problem, and a 36-hour sea journey is preferable to a drive through Spain, take the boat from Sete in France to Tangier. **Southern Ferries** Ⓣ (UK) 0844 815 7785 Ⓦ www.southernferries.co.uk

Package deals

There are over a hundred UK-based operators that offer tours to Morocco, of which more than a dozen provide short-break options to Marrakech. Among the many is **Thomas Cook Holidays** Ⓣ (UK) 0871 895 0055 Ⓦ www.thomascook.com

ENTRY FORMALITIES

There are no visa requirements for stays of up to three months for citizens of the following regions: Australia, Canada, the European Union (including the UK), New Zealand and the USA. South Africans, and foreign nationals residing in the above regions, need to contact their embassies or consulates for further information. All visitors require a passport that is valid for at least six months after their date of entry into Morocco.

Personal effects, including cameras (for non-commercial use) are allowed into the country duty free. Adults are allowed to bring in one bottle of wine and one bottle of spirits. The tobacco allowance is 200 cigarettes, or 50 cigars or 250 grams of tobacco.

MONEY

The dirham is the official currency in Morocco. One dirham equals 100 centimes, although finding things to buy for denominations of less than 1 dirham is rare. Coins come in 5, 10, 20 and 50 centimes, and 1, 5 and 10 dirham. Notes come in units of 20, 50, 100 and 200 dirham.

Moroccan money is not allowed out of the country and should be purchased on arrival and resold (if any is left) before departure. Make sure all exchange is done officially at banks, bureaux de change and hotel cashiers, rather than illegally on the street, especially with traveller's cheques. Receipts issued on the initial transaction are required when changing money back. EU currency is commonly accepted, especially when buying items at the souks, and prices are often quoted in euros.

Most towns have banks that almost always include exchange bureaux. ATMs are reasonably common, especially in the cities. On weekends, both locals and tourists line up at the available cash dispensers, so try to make sure your money supply is topped up during regular banking hours.

Credit cards are accepted at many of the finer hotels, restaurants and shops. Even some souk stalls will take them, and their use can become part of the bartering process – if you are too keen on the item and the seller knows you are dependent on the credit, the price may not be very negotiable. At the same time, if you're unsure about the item and the seller is not flexible, it's very easy to walk away and find someone else who is happier taking the card.

HEALTH, SAFETY & CRIME

Morocco is reasonably safe, and a visit poses no particular heath risk. There are no vaccinations suggested for people either going to, or coming from, the country, and anti-malaria prophylactics are not needed.

However, even though tap water is treated, it's best to drink bottled water. Also, do not drink water from rivers, even fast-flowing mountain streams. Fruit and vegetables should be washed and, where possible, peeled.

Sun protection is important, especially during the summer. Make sure you use suntan cream or block and that you have enough to last for the entire stay. Don't spend too long outdoors, particularly at midday. At all times of the year, swim only in hotel pools, secure beaches and safe areas of coastline.

Morocco adheres to the Islamic beliefs of hospitality and respect, without following some of the more militant fundamentalist trends. Western visitors are encouraged and welcomed. Wandering around Marrakech tends to be very safe, even for women. However, there are always some basic rules that ought to be followed. Dress should be dignified while in the city and especially the Medina. Avoid wearing clothes that are appropriate only for the swimming pool or the beach. At the same time, don't overdress, or wear too much jewellery, and don't carry more money than is necessary for a day out.

It's easy to get lost, particularly at night, but try to avoid areas that are poorly lit. If confused, ask for directions before entering a dark and deserted area.

Police

There has been a strong effort to reduce road accidents in Morocco and as a result, there is radar surveillance in many places, particularly on the road from Marrakech to Essaouira. Be warned that to a Moroccan traffic cop, 60 kph (37 mph) means exactly that. Fines are heavy and are paid directly to the police officer. In addition to regular police, there are also undercover tourist police looking for non-licensed guides and other tourist hazards.

OPENING HOURS

Banks are open 08.15–15.45 and post offices 08.30–16.30 Monday to Friday, both closing at weekends. Business hours are generally 08.00–12.00, 14.00–18.30 Monday to Thursday and 08.00–11.00, 15.00–18.30 on Fridays. Government offices tend to close earlier, around 15.30.

Shops set their own hours, but usually the larger stores are open 09.00–13.00, 15.00–19.00 every day except Sunday. Supermarkets open on Sundays and have longer opening hours, from 08.00–22.00. The merchants in the souks take any opportunity to make money and function 08.00–13.00, 14.00–18.00 every day.

TOILETS

Public toilets are not common, and it's usually best to stop at a decent café, or even a hotel. The attendant will expect a tip. Try to carry a packet of tissues, as away from the better places it's up to you to provide the supply. Plumbing is poor, and the basket you see next to the toilet is for used paper. The facilities at the airport are fine.

CHILDREN

The city's hypermarket, Marjane, on the route de Casablanca, has the largest selection of things for children. The souks are full of goods and colours that fascinate visitors of all ages, and it's possible to find a toy or item that will delight little ones, although the closeness of the markets may be a little frightening. Moroccans love children so don't be surprised if they give your son or daughter a friendly pat on the head, offer pieces of candy or coo over your baby. On Friday and Sunday, both children and adults like feeding the gigantic carp in the reservoir at the Royal Palace's Agdal Gardens.

The Jemaa el Fna is full of attractions for everyone. The hustle and bustle of the city's main square provides entertainment throughout the day but really comes to life at night. Children will love the dancers, singers and magicians and the whole family will appreciate the colour and animation that are generated as the day progresses.

Calèche rides are fun for kids as well as for parents, and the carriages can take a whole family at one time. The hop-on, hop-off sightseeing bus (see page 65) runs tours in colourful double-decker buses – the top deck open-air seating is especially enjoyable for children. Camel rides may also be had in the Palmeraie and on the beach in Essaouira. Essaouira also offers horseback riding and all manner of water sports for children in the summer.

There are a number of playgrounds. The Jardin El Harti in Guéliz has two facing slides disguised as dinosaurs having a head-to-head. The Centre du Kawkab, just down the street from the Jardin El Harti, has two floors of entertainment for children; the ground floor has a play area with a small train ride, trampoline, and climbing maze, good for ages up to eight. Downstairs there are arcade games, a pool table and other activities for bigger kids.

The Station Afriquia gas stations on the route de Casablanca, near the Palmearie and the route to Fez, have good child-friendly restaurants with large playgrounds with zip-lines, climbing jungle gyms and swings surrounded by lots of sand. Good for a few hours of entertainment.

Oasiria (ⓐ route du Barrage, km 4 ⓣ 024 38 04 38 ⓦ www.oasiria.com ⓛ 10.00–18.00 ⓝ Shuttle bus from Jemaa el Fna, Gueliz & pl. el Harti), an expansive outdoor water park, is a great place for kids and adults alike to spend a hot summer's day. Water slides, a wave pool and a river ride which snakes through long channels are just a few of the attractions. Relax on grassy areas or under shady trees. There is a restaurant with pizzas, sandwiches and cold drinks. In winter, there is an outdoor heated pool.

There is always a children's film playing at the Mégarama movie theatre (see page 112). The fact that most are in French can be presented as a cultural bonus to the eager young linguist.

COMMUNICATIONS

Internet

Using the internet is becoming very popular, with access available all over Morocco. Many hotels offer connections as part of their services, sometimes wireless. Outside, access points are advertised on the streets, often alongside the teleboutiques. A few cyber points are:

Café Atlas ⓐ rue de Bab Agnaou, Kissaria Essalam

Café du Livre With Wi-Fi, as well as delicious food and a wide selection of English-language books, this may just be the best place in the city to connect to the internet if you are travelling with your laptop. ⓐ 44 rue Tarik Ben Ziyad ⓣ 05 24 43 21 49 ⓛ 09.00–21.00 Mon–Sat

Cyber Parc Just across from the Hotel de Ville (City Hall), this beautifully landscaped park is equipped with internet access screens that work with phone cards. Not good for surfing at night, but a pleasure to do so by day. ⓐ Arsat Moulay Abdeslam on av. Mohammed V

Phone

Phone numbers in Morocco have recently added a digit: '5' before fixed line numbers and '6' before mobile phone numbers. In old leaflets or directories, you may come across phone numbers such as ☏ 024 12 34 56. This should now be ☏ 05 24 12 34 56. The area code for Marrakech is 05 24.

Payphones work with phone cards that are sold at kiosks and tourist shops around town. Teleboutiques are also very common. Marked outside by a blue sign, these privately run shops have individual secluded booths and a person is on hand to offer change and advice. Prices are very reasonable and it's often easier to find these boutiques than a public phone. Mobile phones function if they are compatible with Morocco's two GSM networks. The national networks have excellent coverage throughout the country.

TELEPHONING MOROCCO

To call Morocco from abroad, dial the local international code then 212. Dropping the first zero listed for domestic calls, dial the local code then the number. For example, to call the Marrakech Tourist Office from within Morocco you should dial ☏ 05 24 43 62 39, or ☏ 00 212 5 24 43 62 39 from the UK.

TELEPHONING ABROAD

To dial abroad from Morocco, first dial the outgoing international code of 00, then the country code. For Australia, it's 61, for Canada and the USA, 1, for the Irish Republic 353, for New Zealand 64, for South Africa 27 and for the UK 44. Dial 120 for international phone enquiries and 160 for national enquiries.

Post

Marrakech's main post office is in Guéliz, at place 16 du Novembre, along avenue Mohammed V. There is a smaller branch in the Medina on rue Moulay Ismail, between the Jemaa el Fna and the Koutoubia. Post offices are open from 08.30–16.30 Monday to Friday and are closed at weekends. Local kiosks and tourist shops also sell stamps. Post boxes are yellow and marked 'Poste'. Packages must be brought to the post office and the contents shown before posting.

ELECTRICITY

Electricity is generally 220 volts AC, 50 Hertz, although some older buildings and small rural villages still work on 110 volts. Plugs have two round pins, as used on the Continent. UK appliances will require an adaptor, while US appliances which work on 110 volts will also require a transformer.

TRAVELLERS WITH DISABILITIES

Marrakech is not particularly easy for tourists with disabilities, as the streets in the Medina are rough, often unpaved and crowded, and traffic is busy all over the city. The newer, larger hotels should have at least one adapted guest room but make sure you explain your needs clearly before arriving. If you have some mobility but struggle with stairs, consider staying in a traditional *riad*, as these have ground-floor rooms set around a central courtyard.

For general information on accessible travel, contact the UK-based organisation **RADAR** (ⓦ www.radar.org.uk) or US-based **SATH** (ⓦ www.sath.org).

TOURIST INFORMATION

Marrakech The city's main tourist office is located in the heart

🔵 *Bureaux de tabac are the places for a postcard or newspaper*

of Guéliz. However, the office is of limited use and they rarely answer their phone. ⓐ pl. Abdelmoumen Ben Ali ⓣ 05 24 43 62 39
Essaouira The local and regional tourist office is located just inside the city walls. ⓐ 10 rue de Caire ⓣ 05 24 78 35 32

Websites
There are many excellent websites describing Marrakech, its sights, *riads* and restaurants. Some of them are:
ⓦ www.ilove-marrakech.com
ⓦ www.madein-marrakech.com
ⓦ www.marrakechpocket.com
ⓦ www.moroccanmaryam.typepad.com
ⓦ www.morocco.com
ⓦ www.riadsmorocco.com

BACKGROUND READING
Many classic works are from writers who have passed through and been inspired by Morocco and its charms. A few are:
Hideous Kinky by Esther Freud. This semi-autobiographical work about being an English child in 1970s Marrakech was turned into a film by Giles MacKinnon.
Naked Lunch by William Burroughs. A controversial, drug-centred classic, this was written while the writer was living in Morocco in the 1950s.
The Sheltering Sky by Paul Bowles. This beautiful and chilling novel, written in 1949, was made into an equally impressionable film by Bernardo Bertolucci in 1990.
The Voices of Marrakech by Elias Canetti. The author wrote this poignant series of stories about his visit 14 years before winning the Nobel Prize for Literature.

Emergencies

Ambulance ℹ 05 24 40 14 01
Doctor (24 hr) ℹ 05 24 40 40 40
Fire brigade (*Pompiers*) ℹ 15 or 05 24 43 04 15
Highway emergency services ℹ 19
Medical emergencies (*Urgences médicales*) ℹ 070 41 95 77,
05 24 40 40 40
Police ℹ 19

MEDICAL SERVICES

All doctors and dentists speak French and a few speak English.
Ask at the tourist office, your hotel or *riad*, or at the consulate.

Dentist (English-speaking)
Dr Youssef Dassouli ⓐ Residence Asmae, apt 6, 1st floor
ℹ (emergency) 06 64 90 65 14

Hospitals
Clinic al Koutoubia ⓐ rue de Paris, Hivernage ℹ 05 24 43 85 85
Polyclinic du Sud ⓐ rue de Yougoslavie, Guéliz ℹ 05 24 44 79 99
Pharmacy (24 hr) ⓐ Jemaa el Fna, next to the police station

POLICE

Police are ever-present in Marrakech's new city and around the Medina's
Jemaa el Fna, with a 24-hour police station directly on the Jemaa el Fna
square. Generally friendly to tourists and easily approachable, some
police officers speak basic English. In the case of a serious problem,
the emergency police number is ℹ 19. Thefts and lost property should
be reported to the Brigade Touristique (Tourist Police) ℹ 05 24 38 46 01.

EMERGENCY PHRASES

Help!	**Fire!**	**Stop!**
Au secours!	Au feu!	Stop!
Ossercoor!	*Oh fur!*	*Stop!*

Call an ambulance/a doctor/the police/the fire service!
Appelez une ambulance/un médecin/la police/les pompiers!
Ahperleh ewn ahngbewlahngss/ang medesang/lah poleess/
leh pompeeyeh!

EMBASSIES & CONSULATES

There is a **British Honorary Consul** in Marrakech ⓐ Residence Jaib 55, blvd Zerktouni ⓣ 05 24 43 50 95 (emergencies only)

Closest embassies are located at:

Australia ⓐ 4 rue Jean Rey, 75724 Cedex 15, Paris, France
ⓣ 33 1 4059 3300 ⓦ www.france.embassy.gov.au

Canada ⓐ 13 bis rue Jaafar Assadik, Rabat ⓣ 05 37 68 74 00
ⓦ www.dfait-maeci.gc.ca

New Zealand ⓐ calle del Pinar 7, 28006 Madrid, Spain
ⓣ 34 915 230 226 ⓦ www.nzembassy.com

South Africa ⓐ 34 rue des Saadiens, Rabat ⓣ 05 37 70 67 60
ⓦ www.dfa.gov.za

UK ⓐ 17 av. de la Tour Hassan, Rabat ⓣ 05 37 63 33 33
ⓦ www.britishembassy.gov.uk

USA ⓐ 2 av. de Marrakesh, Rabat ⓣ 05 37 76 22 65
ⓦ www.usembassy.ma

Editorial/project management: Lisa Plumridge
Copy editor: Monica Guy
Layout/DTP: Alison Rayner

The publishers would like to thank the following individuals and organisations for supplying their copyright photographs for this book: Rene August, page 59; Bains de Marrkaech, page 57; Jonatha Borzicchi/ BigStockPhoto.com, page 31; Jonatha Borzicchi/Dreamstime.com, page 11; Dar Moha, page 93; Les Jardins de la Koutoubia/Yohan Hervé, page 94; iStockphoto.com (Lorna Piche, pages 50–1; naphtalina, page 104; Brian Raisbeck, page 99; Izaokas Sapiro, page 128–9); Javier Lastras, page 9; Maryam Montague, pages 27, 33, 54, 67, 90, 136; C Redecke, page 133; Stockxpert.com (Willaume Gautier, page 86; irabel8, pages 5 & 143; Richard Waters, page 25); SXC.hu (Susannah Huntington, page 71; Caroline Keyzor, page 77; Alcide Nikopol, pages 36–7); Ethel Davies, all others.

Send your thoughts to
books@thomascook.com

- Found a great bar, club, shop or must-see sight that we don't feature?

- Like to tip us off about any information that needs a little updating?

- Want to tell us what you love about this handy little guidebook and more importantly how we can make it even handier?

Then here's your chance to tell all! Send us ideas, discoveries and recommendations today and then look out for your valuable input in the next edition of this title.

Email the above address (stating the title) or write to: pocket guides Series Editor, Thomas Cook Publishing, PO Box 227, Coningsby Road, Peterborough PE3 8SB, UK.